D0405385

Like I'm the Only Squirrel in the World

COLLECTION EDITOR: **JENNIFER GRÜNWALD**
ASSISTANT EDITOR: **CAITLIN O'CONNELL**
ASSOCIATE MANAGING EDITOR: **KATERI WOODY**
EDITOR, SPECIAL PROJECTS: **MARK D. BEAZLEY**
VP PRODUCTION & SPECIAL PROJECTS: **JEFF YOUNGQUIST**
SVP PRINT, SALES & MARKETING: **DAVID GABRIEL**
BOOK DESIGNER: **JAY BOWEN**

EDITOR IN CHIEF: **AXEL ALONSO**
CHIEF CREATIVE OFFICER: **JOE QUESADA**
PUBLISHER: **DAN BUCKLEY**
EXECUTIVE PRODUCER: **ALAN FINE**

THE UNBEATABLE SQUIRREL GIRL VOL. 5: LIKE I'M THE ONLY SQUIRREL IN THE WORLD. Contains material originally published in magazine form as THE UNBEATABLE SQUIRREL GIRL #12-16. First printing 2017. ISBN# 978-1-302-90328-2. Published by MARVEL WORLDWIDE, INC., a subsidiary of MARVEL ENTERTAINMENT, LLC. OFFICE OF PUBLICATION: 135 West 50th Street, New York, NY 10020. Copyright © 2017 MARVEL. No similarity between any of the names, characters, persons, and/or institutions in this magazine with those of any living or dead person or institution is intended, and any such similarity which may exist is purely coincidental. **Printed in Canada.** ALAN FINE, President, Marvel Entertainment; DAN BUCKLEY, President, TV, Publishing & Brand Management; JOE QUESADA, Chief Creative Officer; TOM BREVOORT, SVP of Publishing; DAVID BOGART, SVP of Business Affairs & Operations, Publishing & Partnership; C.B. CEBULSKI, VP of Brand Management & Development, Asia; DAVID GABRIEL, SVP of Sales & Marketing, Publishing; JEFF YOUNGQUIST, VP of Production & Special Projects; DAN CARR, Executive Director of Publishing Technology; ALEX MORALES, Director of Publishing Operations; SUSAN CRESPI, Production Manager; STAN LEE, Chairman Emeritus. For information regarding advertising in Marvel Comics or on Marvel.com, please contact Vit DeBellis, Integrated Sales Manager, at vdebellis@marvel.com. For Marvel subscription inquiries, please call 888-511-5480. **Manufactured between 1/27/2017 and 2/28/2017 by SOLISCO PRINTERS, SCOTT, QC, CANADA.**

10 9 8 7 6 5 4 3 2 1

Ryan North
WRITER

Will Murray
WRITER, 15-YEAR-OLD DOREEN SEQUENCE

Erica Henderson
ARTIST

Rico Renzi
COLOR ARTIST

Anthony Clark *(#13)*, **Hannah Blumenreich** *(#13)* & **Michael Cho** *(#15)*
TRADING CARD ART

Zac Gorman
MEW'S DREAM COMICS ART

Steve Ditko
DOREEN'S COSTUME DRAWING ART

VC's Clayton Cowles
LETTERER

Erica Henderson
COVER ART

Charles Beacham
ASSISTANT EDITOR

Wil Moss
EDITOR

SPECIAL THANKS TO **CK RUSSELL**

SQUIRREL GIRL CREATED BY **WILL MURRAY** & **STEVE DITKO**

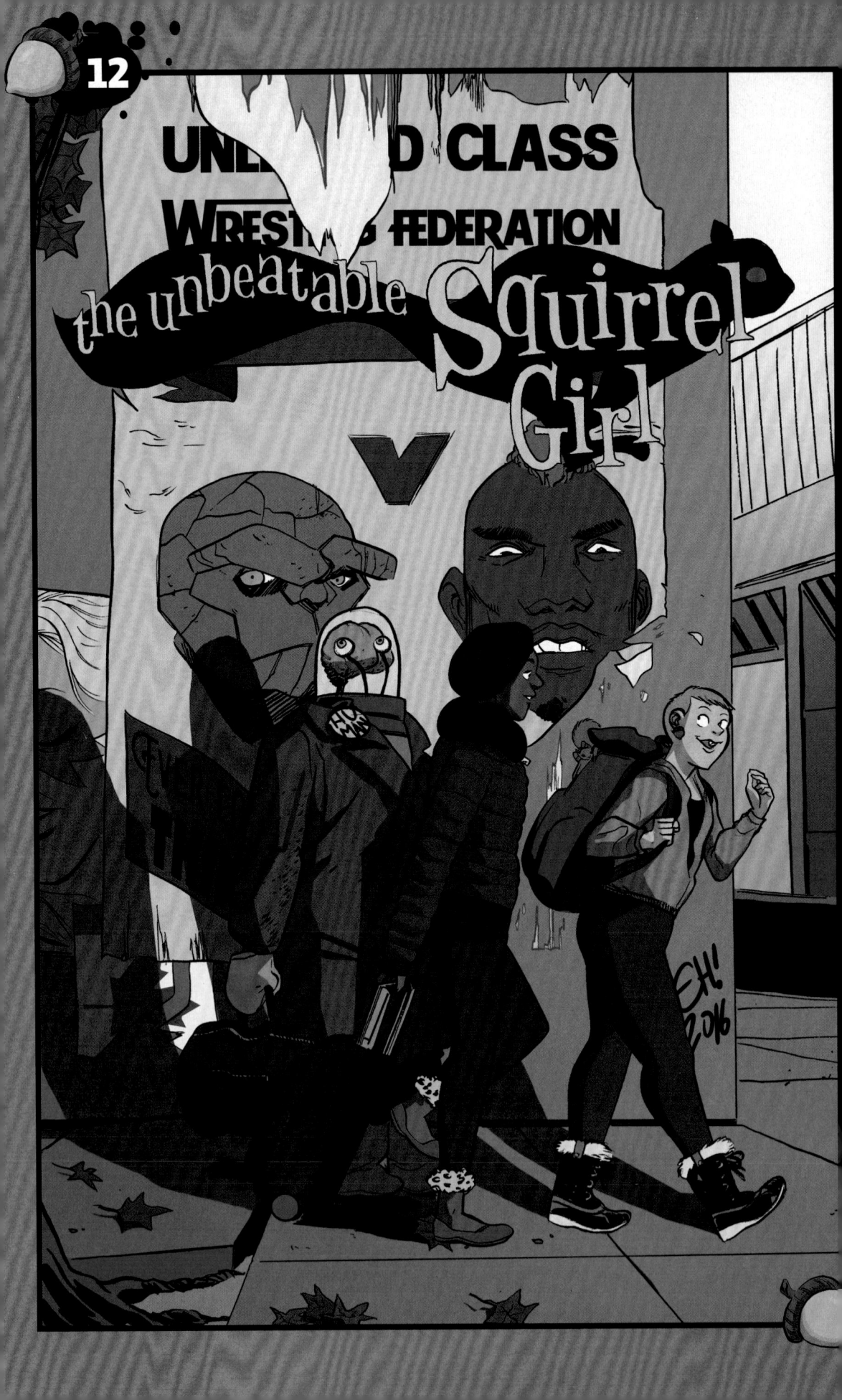
UNL D CLASS
WRESTL G FEDERATION
the unbeatable Squirrel Girl
V
EH!
2016

Doreen Green isn't just a second-year computer science student: she secretly also has all the powers of both squirrel and girl! She uses her amazing abilities to fight crime **and** be as awesome as possible. You know her as...**The Unbeatable Squirrel Girl!** Find out what she's been up to, with...

Squirrel Girl *in a nutshell*

Squirrel Girl @unbeatablesg
Whew, I just had THE BEST NIGHT'S SLEEP OF ALL TIME. For some reason I feel like I could take on the world?

Squirrel Girl @unbeatablesg
Like, I woke up energized and jazzed, as if I really had just defeated a super villain and saved the world...IN MY SLEEP!! Felt great tbh

Squirrel Girl @unbeatablesg
But hah hah that's impossible so oh well

Spider-Man @aspidercan
@unbeatablesg actually there's a doctor strange bad guy named "nightmare" that you could've technically fought in your dreams!!!

Spider-Man @aspidercan
@unbeatablesg doc strange isn't on here though otherwise we could ask him

Squirrel Girl @unbeatablesg
@aspidercan A guy with a doctorate in strangeness doesn't hang out online here? WEIRD

Squirrel Girl @unbeatablesg
@aspidercan YOU'D THINK HE'D FIT RIGHT IN

Tony Stark @starkmantony
@unbeatablesg Hey, how's that robot brain in a jar guy you patched up working out?

Squirrel Girl @unbeatablesg
@starkmantony Brain Drain? Great! Well on his way to becoming a real hero, actually! Still mega nihilistic but in a cool way

Squirrel Girl @unbeatablesg
@starkmantony We're going out on patrol together in a bit actually

Tony Stark @starkmantony
@unbeatablesg Shouldn't you not mention when you're going out on patrol, so the criminal element won't know?

Squirrel Girl @unbeatablesg
@starkmantony good point my dude, one sec

Squirrel Girl @unbeatablesg
HELLO CRIMINALS, THIS IS JUST TO ANNOUNCE THAT I AM ON PATROL ALWAYS AND WILL DEFINITELY CATCH YOU DOING A CRIME, SO DON'T DO THEM

Spider-Man @aspidercan
@unbeatablesg holy crap can i use that

Squirrel Girl @unbeatablesg
@starkmantony Tony are you there I just had the best idea!! Tony tony tony

Tony Stark @starkmantony
@unbeatablesg Hey.

Squirrel Girl @unbeatablesg
@starkmantony TONY. BRAINSTORM. What if you changed your name from "Tony Stark" to--HEAR ME OUT--..."Ira."

Tony Stark @starkmantony
@unbeatablesg "Ira Stark"?

Squirrel Girl @unbeatablesg
@starkmantony IRA ONMANN.

Tony Stark @starkmantony
@unbeatablesg oh my god

Squirrel Girl @unbeatablesg
@starkmantony Tony I'm going on vacation so I just wanted to give you something to remember me by

Squirrel Girl @unbeatablesg
@starkmantony just a little memento

Squirrel Girl @unbeatablesg
@starkmantony for my good friend

Squirrel Girl @unbeatablesg
@starkmantony ira onmann

search!

#braindrain
#canada
#nopowernoproblems
#maureengreen

These are the bank robbers from the first time Squirrel Girl saved a bank! They're back! And they're still robbing banks! Wow, I'd really hoped they'd have worked towards positive change in their own lives but *hah hah hah* ***guess not!***

Brain Drain's costume displays a crime-fighting algorithm right there on its chest! Every criminal who sees it and executes that pseudocode will find their lives improved! This is next-level costume design!!

Larry was the bank robber way back in our first volume's #3! Fun Larry Fact: his interests include both getting money for free ***and*** recidivism. Not a good look on you, Larry!

TSA agents freak out even if you wear shoes when you're not supposed to! They are clearly not yet woke enough for tails.

And I got new shades at a doll store for extremely stylish dolls! Are we ready? We're wasting prime lake time!

Last chance! Everyone's got everything they need? Teleporter's one-way, and it's gonna be a long bus ride back to NYC if we forget something.

So ready, Doreen!

Anything I forgot I will build out of sticks and leaves.

Okay, teleporter engaged!

KLIK

So assuming nothing goes ***catastrophically wrong, ha ha ha,*** the next thing you see will be--

VZZHHNNN

Other email autoresponses that have no possible downsides include "haha seriously?? tell me more!!", "interesting, let's follow up on this tomorrow!", and "who are you and how did you get this email?". Like I said, no possible downsides!!

Also I'm sorry I mentioned catastrophic failures as we were literally stepping into a teleporter: that was bad timing and I apologize. It was really just a completely catastrophic failure of timing on my part. ...Sorry again.

I had plans to "like" some criminal's tweets and then when they saw my "like" they'd freak out and stop doing crimes, due to insecurity about my all-seeing social media game. I had *plans*, Nancy.

You can also take out our new book from the library! You might think that people in the business of selling books would be against places where you can read books for free, but here is a secret: libraries are awesome, librarians are even *more* awesome, and both are among the greatest things civilization has given us. *No apologies; it's true.*

I tried to make all these magazines sound boring, but man, I would totally read 100% of these magazines. Large scale *mega-boring?* Now *that's* an infrastructure development project whose industry insider details I'm curious to learn more about!

=Sigh= You and me both, Brain Drain.

Brain Drain has trouble telling humans apart, but can remember their names with the efficiency of a robot man. In contrast, I can distinguish between ***thousands*** of people whose names I've long ago forgotten and now it's way way ***way*** too late to ask. Life is full of challenges, everyone!!

Squirrel Girl has learned a lot about herself on this trip, primarily that she has a super-weakness to getting bored when there's nothing to do and no internet around. Keep it a secret, okay? Friends don't spread their friends' super-weaknesses around!!

Alternative titles for this case: "The Case of the Cupcake Caper," "Just Desserts," and "The Mysterious Muffin of Skellington Bay" (did you know: if a bay doesn't have a name you can ***probably*** just name that bay??)

HOWEVER I HAVE BEEN TOLD THAT SOMETIMES THE SURPRISES ARE KITTENS AND ICE CREAM, SO I HOLD OUT HOPE, EVER DREAMING OF THE ICE CREAM KITTEN IN MY FUTURE

Most squirrels are red/green colorblind, which means they have trouble telling red and green apart. If you share this property too, then good news! You have at least one *squirrel super-power*, and that's more than most people can say!

Honestly: I'm not sure what I was expecting, but I feel confident in saying that "a tiny village beneath the floorboards" is the polar opposite of that.

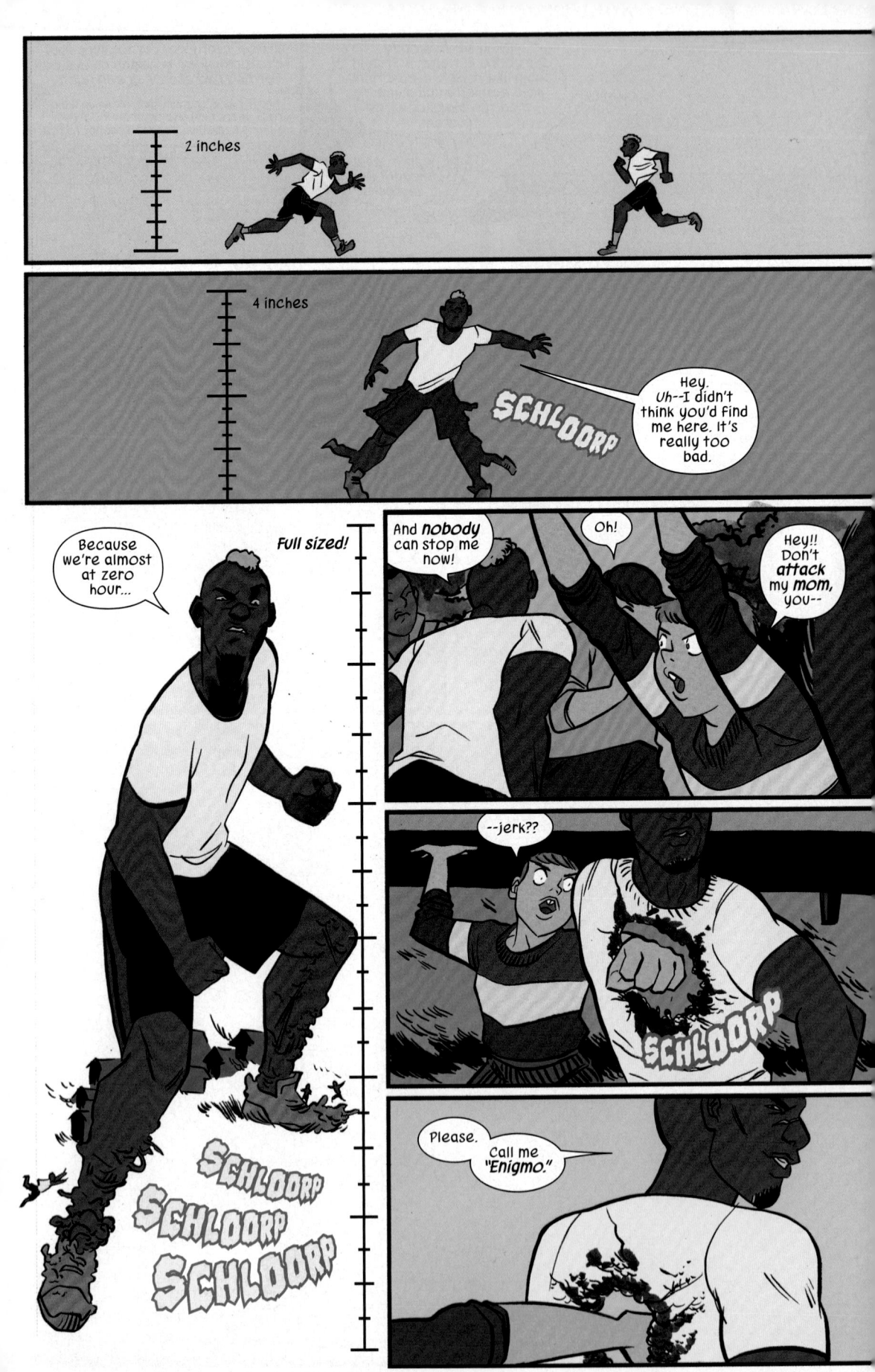

Enigmo. No, like "enigma," but with an "o." Enigmo. Look, do you have a pen? I can write it--no, it's not "Edward Nigmo"! You're thinking of another guy, and you're not even remembering him that accurately!!

Well, looks like that's it for NYC! But now let's cut back to what everyone's really concerned about: the quiet northern nation of Canada!!

Gah!!

So irresponsible, dude!!
Don't punch someone carrying a house!

Okay, hit him and he splits into tiny dudes who continue to attack you. Maybe I can...
SCHLOORP
...um...

Uh...

SMAK

Uh... any ideas, guys?

...guys??
Hey! Hey!
Not into this! Definitely not into this!

KIK
KIK
KIK

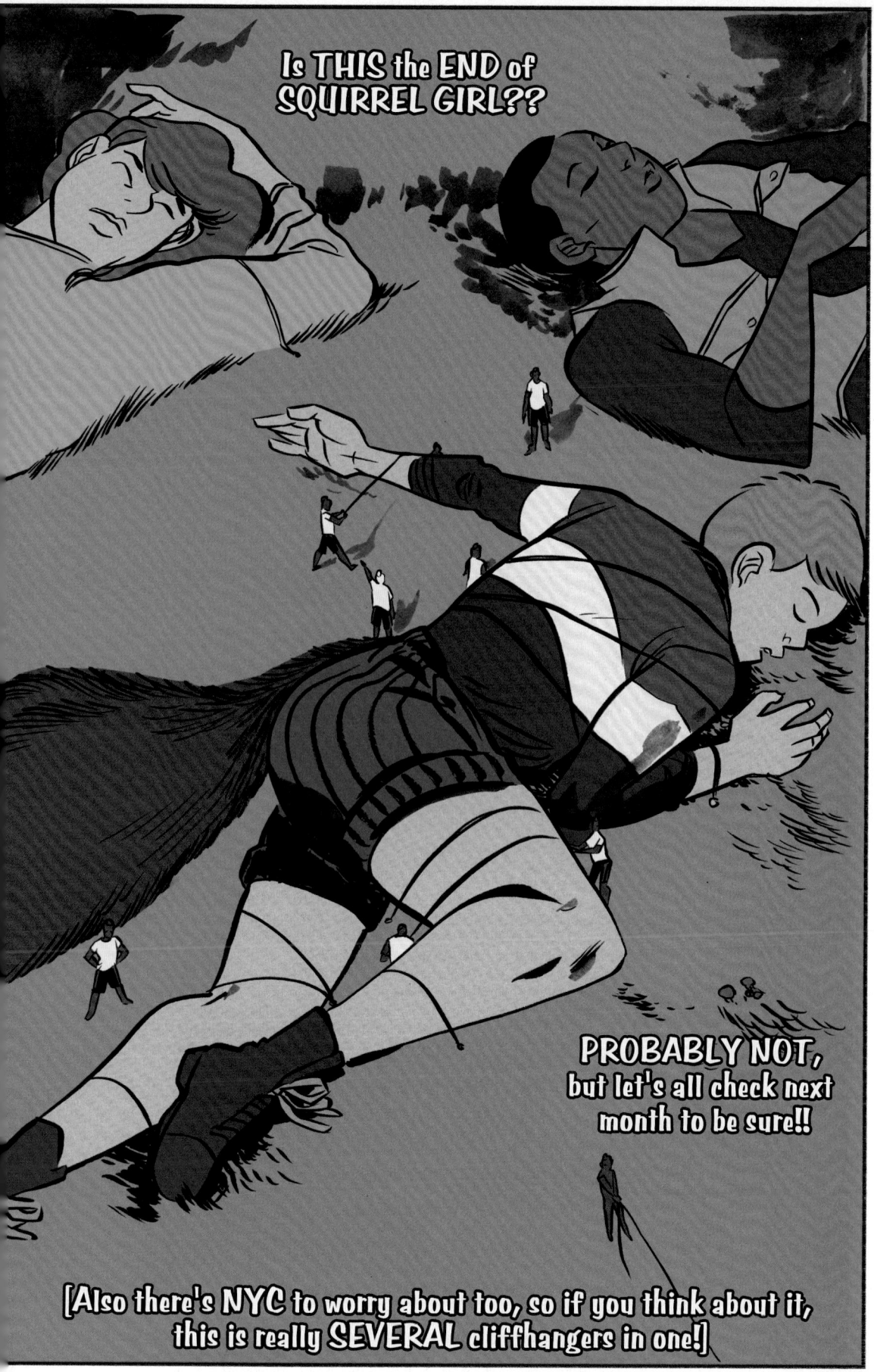

Plus we're gonna have a guest star next month! His identity might be a...*tiny* bit surprising?

Letters From Nuts

Ryan!

Erica!

Send letters to mheroes@marvel.com or 135 W 50th St, 7th Floor, New York, NY 10020 (Please mark "OKAY TO PRINT"

Hey, Squirrelly Friends!

I just got done reading SG #11, and I feel like every new issue reminds me how much I love this friggin' series! This issue had everything that makes SQUIRREL GIRL so unique and enjoyable, from the rad humor to the organic way that you weave fun facts and actual computer science terms into the story in a plot-relevant way.

Which actually brings me to a point! (Yay for segues!) I should preface this by saying that I totally understand that you were going for a computer science angle on this, but would you believe me if I told you that there is an even more efficient way to count on one hand? It's true, dudes! In American Sign Language, you can actually count up to 999 before having to bring in a second hand! Pretty neat, right?

Anyway, I loved, loved, loved the issue, and I cannot wait to see Erica and Ryan at NYCC this year. Keep being your awesome selves!

Peace out, Squirrel Scouts,
Shani

RYAN: I know a bit of ASL and I considered mentioning that style of finger-counting, but it didn't fit the computer science theme of the issue! Alas. You already know this, Shani, but guess what, everyone else? ASL is an amazing language. When my wife and I are at a party and we want to see if the other one wants to go home, we sometimes catch the other's eye and discreetly sign "GO [to] HOUSE?" It's really easy: you can sign "GO" by pointing your index fingers on each hand at each other and rotating them around each other in a rolling motion, and "HOUSE" is just making your hands form the roof of a house and then bringing them down for the walls. Do it really quick and nobody will even know you're the kind of person who leaves a party to go home because you get sleepy sometimes! Technically we should be saying "GO HOME?" but the sign for HOME is less discreet.

ERICA: Hey guys, I know a lot about computer science and sign language as well! Just don't ask me any questions about them. What fun we're having talking about things we all know about. Anyway, did you know that New York Comic Con will be the FIRST TIME Ryan and I are doing a convention together??

Dear Erica and Ryan,

I have been reading and re-reading SQUIRREL GIRL many times over the last month or two, and am on a bit of a squirre(vangelica)l mission to share its wonders with my comics-loving friends.

I stayed at a lovely place called Looking Stead in the Lake District (UK) last weekend where RED SQUIRRELS ARE AN ACTUAL FEATURE. Attached is a pic of my view at breakfast.

I have no idea if she's capable of kicking butts (crime being somewhat rare in them parts), but the other half of the theme song still seems to hold true.

P.S. The "squirrel" homonym puns don't work that well in the UK due to the difference in pronunciation. We're generally "squi-RUhl" more than "squrl." But that is like the only complaint I have about your comic so just keep being hilarious and I am sorry for bringing it up.

Unless Doreen comes to the UK, in which case IT IS ON (between squirrels, maybe).

Very much love,
Kevin

RYAN: I think Erica and I both SOMETIMES do a deliberate "Squir-RELL Guir-RELL" in the way we've heard people from the UK and Germany try to pronounce it so it rhymes. Two syllables for both "squirrel" and "girl"! It's actually very charming. Also, Kevin: Is crime rare in the parts where you saw the squirrels by chance, or could it be...the squirrels are the ones KEEPING the crime rate low?? Just something to think about in case you're planning to start stealing everyone's stuff in what I can tell you now is the delightful-looking Looking Stead in the Lake District.

ERICA: I love seeing other types of squirrels in the wild. I've always lived on the upper east coast so it's mostly eastern greys for me. Toronto is full of black squirrels. It's so cool. We'll be out in Leeds for the Thought Bubble comic convention later this year. I look forward to seeing what sorts of squirrels that trip will bring.

Dear Nutty Buddies,

After nearly two years, I was beginning to wonder when Erica was going to need a break, and I dreaded the idea of someone else coming along to try and fill her shoes. So let me just say how pleasantly surprised I was with guest artist Jacob Chabot's work in issue #11! And even without his sister from another mister, Ryan knocked another great issue out of the park too, so kudos to both of you. From Doc Ock to Krave the College Administrator, this issue really felt lik an homage to Squirrel Girl co-creator Steve Ditk in so many ways. I mean, if Doreen signaling "s o'clock" in binary hand signs while defeatin one of Doctor Strange's oldest villains, who i turn is wrapped in the symbiotic flesh of one c Spider-Man's most powerful adversaries isn't totally kick-butt tribute to one of Marvel's grea artist-creators, then I don't know what is! An thankfully, Erica wasn't completely absent fron this issue either, and I'm not just talking abou the final panel she drew. Her comment in th letters page about the best ever Nomad phas has secured her the highest place in my esteer for all time. Now, if you could just figure out way to bring him back from the dead, Noma would be in his "Lazarus Lorenzo Lamas" phas which, of course, would be even better!

Darryl Etheridg
St. Catharines, O

P.S. I have to ask, do Doreen and/or Tippy Toe ever watch AMC's *The Walking Dead* and, so, how do they feel about Daryl Dixon's favorit snack?

RYAN: Here is a thing: I wrote this issu because I like to have one-shot issue between arcs where we can try something little different, and it was already complete scripted when we realized Erica woul need time off to focus on the UNBEATABL SQUIRREL GIRL BEATS UP THE MARVE UNIVERSE! book we're working on (which w already mentioned in the comic itself so it's nc like I need to mention it again here BUT STILL And by complete luck, the next issue to b drawn already had a stand-alone story wher a different art style would fit perfectly WITHI the narrative of the comic itself! Even that las panel of Doreen sleeping was already scripte all we changed was to have that one drawn b Erica. So it worked out really well AND Jaco knocked it out of the friggin' park.

As for *The Walking Dead*, I've only playe the Clementine games, so I'll have to defer t Erica's encyclopedia knowledge of televisio on this one.

ERICA: Haha. It wasn't even a break. It wa "OH NO I STILL HAVE HALF OF THIS 105 PAG OGN TO DRAW AND THERE'S THE MONTHL BOOK TOO? WHY DID I AGREE TO THIS?" was sort of the opposite of a break. Anywa luckily I was heading to Heroes Con (run by ou very own Rico Renzi) right as we decided t get a fill-in, so I spent the weekend scoutin I didn't even realize Jacob was there until th

on after-party and he was in my top two to do t. Serendipity!

Interestingly enough, even though I am lways bingeing TV shows and horror movies vhile I work (it just helps having something lse going on while I draw), I never got round to *The Walking Dead*. I haven't even layed the game yet! Ask me any questions bout *Community* or the *Hellraiser* series, hough. Fun Fact: I don't put anything on vhile I do layouts because there's too much ritical thinking there. Movies that I always vork well to: *Resident Evil, Naked Lunch*.

Ryan and Erica,

This is the first letter I have EVER written to omic creators, and it starts out a little funny, ut trust me, it will make sense in a minute. am a huge SG fan, even more so since you wo started working on it. I am also a STAR VARS fan. I have read everything, and I mean verything STAR WARS. Even stuff like the ook where the Emperor's illegitimate triclops on finds the glove of Darth Vader on an nderwater planet and it gives him the ability o use Force Lightning. Now Marvel has STAR VARS and the comics are great, and I love hem. But on the days where USG and a STAR VARS comic come out at the same time, I look t them both. And without ANY hesitation at all, pick up your comic and devour it while Poe ooks on sadly or Luke just sits there waiting or me to get on with his story. I would once gain like to impress how much your comic neans to me and the joy it brings. I have loved TAR WARS since I was 4, about 30 years ow, but now it has to wait so I can see the wesome adventures the Unbeatable, CS-oving Squirrel Girl and her amazing friends are p to. (Also, I can count to 31 on my fingers ow! You guys rock!) Keep up the great work nd May the squirrels be with you!

Brad Woolwine
Austin, TX

RYAN: Aw, Brad, this is great! Thank ou. But now I really want to know about his triclops son and what his deal is. Was e a duoclops like most of us, who just verachieved? A quadroclops who lost an ye? Now I'm gonna have to read the STAR VARS book, "The Tale of the Triclops and the nderwater Lightning Glove," which is what I incerely hope that book was called.

ERICA: Fun Fact: When I was a kid I lways insisted on playing as Han Solo but lso I had a lightsaber (large stick). I think ll of us had lightsabers actually, as long as here were enough sticks.

Hi!

I just wanted to say how much I love your omics! I can see myself in Doreen (and quirrel Girl) and I feel like if I were a super ero, I'd be like her. I am currently working on Squirrel Girl costume for Halloween, despite omehow being "too old for dressing up"... I ean, you can never be too old for free candy, ght? Also, I NEED to see Squirrel Girl say, Quick! To the Squirrel Scooter!" :)

Nina G.
Milwaukee, WI
(P.S. Go Great Lakes Avengers!)

RYAN: Nina, you gotta send us pictures of your costume! You ARE never too old for candy (just ask my friend Joey, who – somehow?? – manages to survive on eating mostly candy) (KIDS: do not do this, there are Consequences) (ADULTS: don't do it either, I don't know how Joey hasn't turned into a giant Swedish Berry by now).

Speaking of the Great Lakes and their avenging thereof, I met Zac Gorman (he's writing the new GREAT LAKES AVENGERS book! It's gonna come out soon!) and we discussed SECRETS about Squirrel Girl, and now I'm super excited to see what the GLA get up to.

ERICA: WHAT? THERE ARE SECRETS? WHY DON'T I KNOW THESE SECRETS? Don't say that it's because they're secret, RYAN. Anyway, it is August as I type this and I'm already stressing out because my fiancé and I haven't planned out our matching Halloween costumes yet, so don't worry. Anyway, cosplay tips: Costume 1 is a halter body suit. Costume 2 is a tennis dress with capri leggings (because I got really excited that they make sports dresses but then I was like "these are so short you're literally jumping around and now everybody has seen your butt").

Ryan,

Some suggestions for Nancy Whitehead catchphrases:

Go for the eyes, Mew!

Stuck with ANSI? Here comes Nancy!

It's time to knit sweaters and pet Mew.

It's time to count stitches and engage in at times heated, albeit always rational, discourse!

Also, does Nancy have a middle name and does it start with "P" because then her catchphrase could be "You've got an NP problem to deal with now, buddy." /slickt/

That sound effect is an HP RPN calculator opening.

Erica, you are perfect in every conceivable way appropriate to the appreciation of your work by an old married man.

Please never stop,
Gary

RYAN: These are all solid catchphrases and I see nothing wrong with any of them! I do like the idea of Nancy taunting a bad guy by saying "Things are about to get hard for you, buddy. NP HARD." Fun Fact: I attended a lecture by Professor Cook – who introduced the P vs NP problem, which remains the greatest open question in computer science – at the University of Toronto! If you ask ME, P does NOT equal NP, but I, uh, don't know how to prove it. For those of us who don't have a ready knowledge of computer research to refer to, know this: Nancy's tagline is extremely excellent and if she ever fought someone who studied computational complexity theory, they would be very impressed by it.

ERICA: Gary is a smart guy. Real smart.

Dear Ryan and Erica,

I'm 9 years old and I LOVE, LOVE, LOVE the SQUIRREL GIRL comics! They're so funny! My dad and I go to our favorite comic book store and buy SQUIRREL GIRL comics along with my mom. I just recently had a SG comic book marathon with my guinea pig, Twix. She jumps around happily while I read out loud to her. Twix is going to be Tippy-Toe, my dad and mom are going to probably be squirrels, and I'll be Squirrel Girl for Halloween. Quick question: Does Twix look a bit like Tippy-Toe? Keep up the great work with these comics!!! (Attached is a picture of Twix.) #<3SG4EVER

Your Squirrel Girl Fans,
Isabel Mendoza and Twix
Las Vegas, Nevada

RYAN: TWIX LOOKS SUPER CUTE AND I CAN DEFINITELY SEE THE RESEMBLANCE. Also I love that you and Twix are going as Squirrel Girl and Tippy, respectively, and your parents are going as unnamed squirrels. That's what they get for not calling more exciting characters sooner!

ERICA: Dear Isabel, please send us pictures of Twix in a little bow. I suggest a tiny clip-on since I think most rodents will not deal well with a ribbon tied around them (Tippy-Toe is not most rodents). Also send us photos of ALL OF YOU IN COSTUME.

Next Issue:

Attention, Squirrel Scouts! Make sure to check out our production blog, **unbeatablesquirrelgirl.tumblr.com**, where we post behind-the-scenes stuff on how the book gets made, along with all sorts of cool things *you* make: fanart, cosplay, whatever!

the unbeatable Squirrel Girl
WHEN ANT-MAN AND TIPPY-TOE AND SQUIRREL GIRL JOIN FORCES,
SOMEONE'S GONNA GET BIT!

oreen Green isn't just a second-year computer science student: she secretly also has all the powers of both squirrel and girl! She uses her amazing abilities to fight crime **and** be as awesome as possible. You know her as...**The Unbeatable Squirrel Girl!** Find out what she's been up to, with...

Squirrel Girl *in a nutshell*

Squirrel Girl @unbeatablesg
guys i'm SO BORED, i'm up here in CANADA but there's NOTHING TO DO except read boring magazines

Squirrel Girl @unbeatablesg
and the magazines are SO BORING that i can no longer use punctuation or capital letters

Squirrel Girl @unbeatablesg
boredom has literally sucked the ability to use punctuation out of me

Squirrel Girl @unbeatablesg
science thought it couldn't be done

Squirrel Girl @unbeatablesg
but here we are

Squirrel Girl @unbeatablesg
me with internet: HI I'M COOL AND CAN DISCUSS SEVERAL INTERESTING SUBJECTS!!!
me without internet: i wonder what bark tastes like

Squirrel Girl @unbeatablesg
me with internet: I HAVE SEVERAL HOT TAKES ABOUT TODAY'S NEWS!!
me without internet: so it's decided: i can sneeze at least 3 different ways

Squirrel Girl @unbeatablesg
me with internet: CAN'T WAIT TO CHILL WITH MY PAL TONY STARK ON SOCIAL MEDIA
me without internet: me and that rock are bffs, don't @ me

Squirrel Girl @unbeatablesg
me with internet: WOW SO THAT'S WHAT MY ROBOT PAL BRAIN DRAIN IS DOING IN NYC!
me without internet: i have unsolicited opinions on gardening

Squirrel Girl @unbeatablesg
UPDATE: guys it's a few hours later and things are more interesting now!! There's a CRIME going on!

Squirrel Girl @unbeatablesg
Someone is stealing muffins from my mom!! It's the CASE of the MISSING MUFFINS and I am ON IT

Squirrel Girl @unbeatablesg
also yes I am aware of how pathetic this sounds but listen, I NEED THIS

Squirrel Girl @unbeatablesg
UPDATE 2: okay it turns out there's a whole city of tiny men living beneath our rental cottage who can split apart and back together

Squirrel Girl @unbeatablesg
and who are attacking us on sight for some reason that I don't know!! WHOA!!

Squirrel Girl @unbeatablesg
Anyway I queued these all to post when I'm back in a place that has FRIGGIN' DATA but I should really get back to it

Squirrel Girl @unbeatablesg
Can't fake being knocked out FOREVER, you know?

Squirrel Girl @unbeatablesg
Plus, these tiny Enigmos who are trying to tie me to the ground aren't gonna let me use my phone indefinitely, I'm pretty sure

search!

#canadafacts

#dontatme

#gardening

#thatsapaddlin

#enigmos

This is the Canadian Forest: quiet, peaceful, serene...that is, until ***Engimo the splitty-apart bad guy*** wakes up! (He's a bad guy who splits apart into smaller bad guys who can also split apart, and how we're all up to speed.)

See, what happens is he gets so small that air can carry him, and then you breathe in Engimo dust, and then you've got tiny Enigmos in your lungs that smush together to form a larger but still pretty tiny Enigmo inside your lungs. *Hard pass.*

Q: How did Doreen avoid being seen? A: She scurried along the ground to the far side of the tree, and then leaped up to the branches, using the trunk as cover! We would've shown it but we've only got so many pages per issue, and we figured y'all already knew the specifics of tree-based stealth! You're ***Squirrel Girl readers.*** You got this!

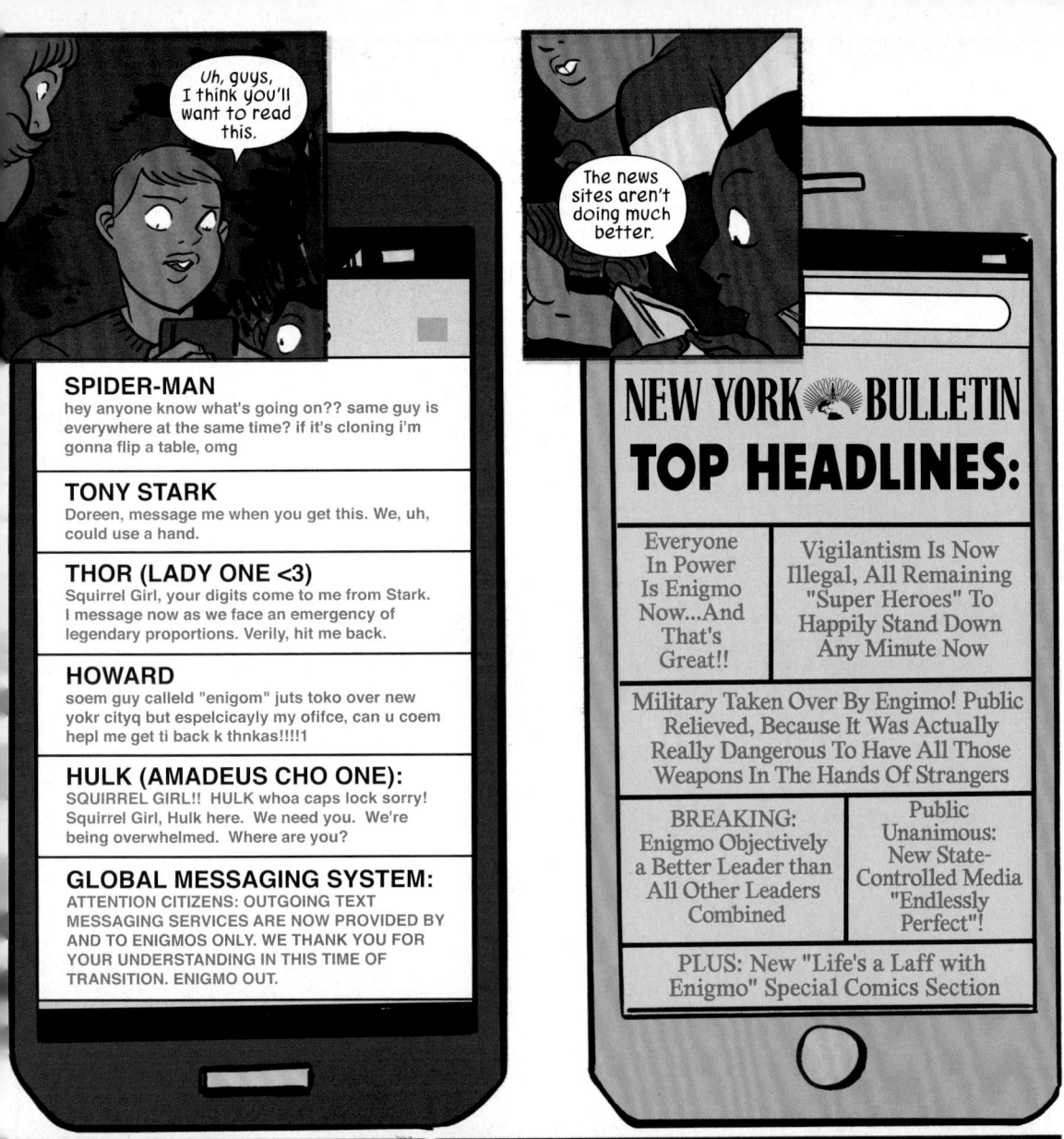

>s he kcikde me in teh btutt adn caleld me "quackres," whikc, like, *heolio* I'ev hearfd rthem all ebfore! I've herads thme alol befoer, sqyulkrel gurl!! waugh!!! anywya hti me bakc

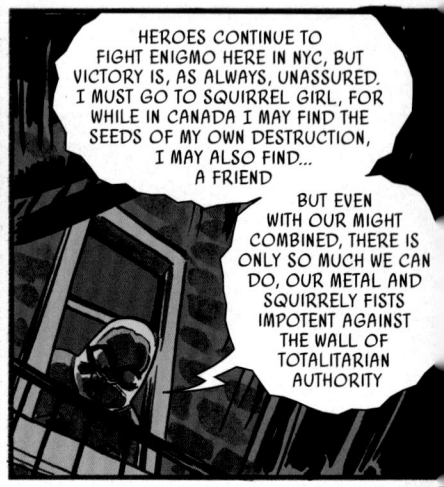

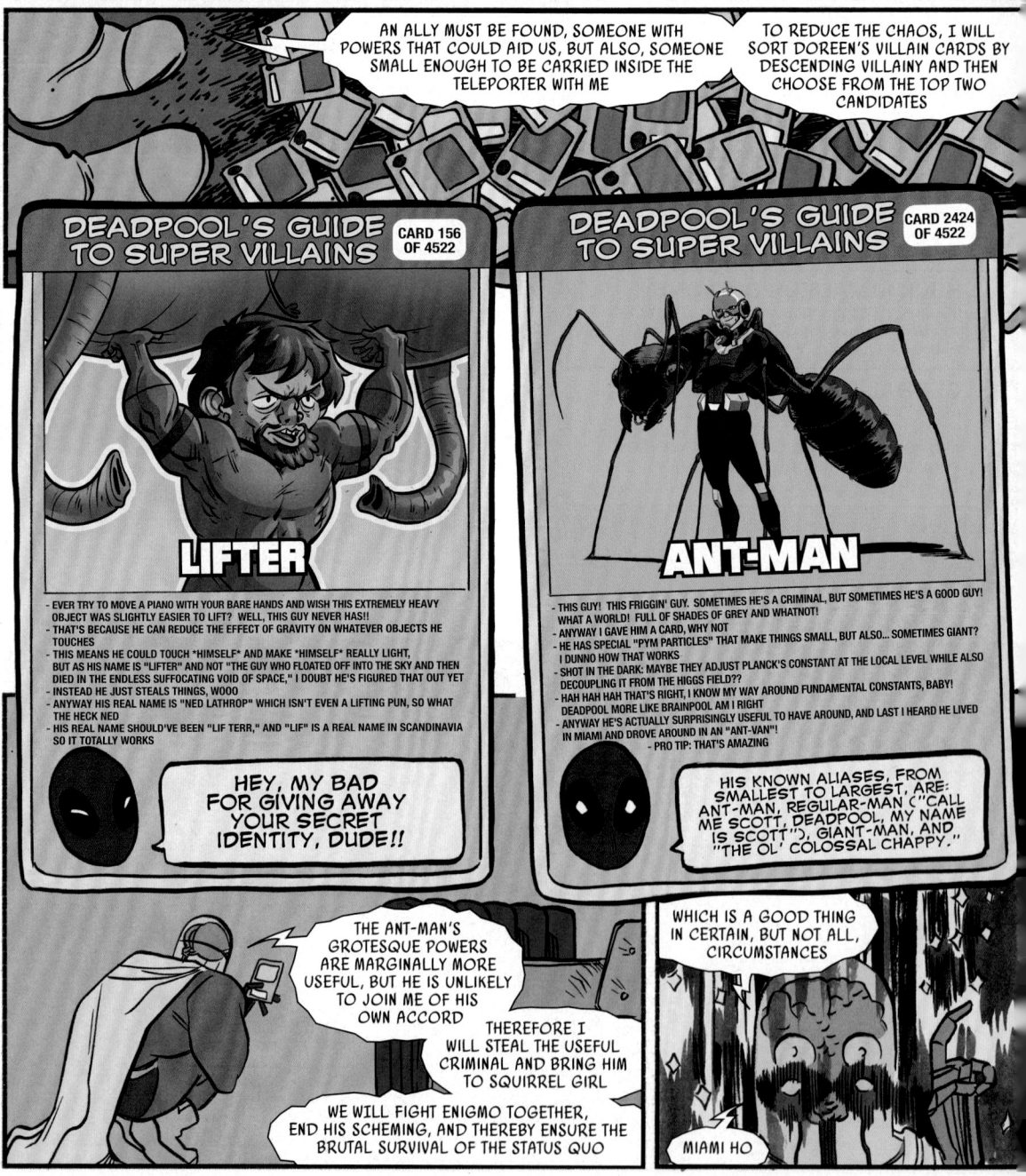

BRAIN DRAIN'S LOG, UPDATE 3X40Fb: ALSO I DON'T LIVE HERE IN DOREEN'S APARTMENT BUT SHE GAVE ME A KEY, SO THAT'S COOL

Those "HNNNNK" and "HNHH" are snoring sound effects. I created them by listening to someone snore as they slept while taking detailed notes!!

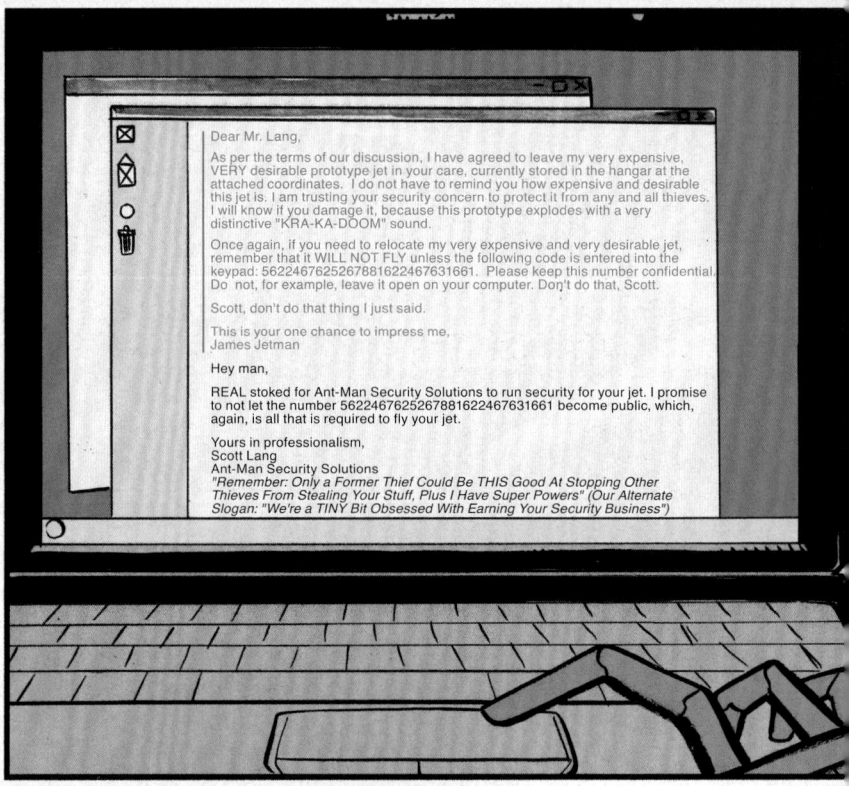

Our Backup Alternate Slogan: "You CAN'T Steal What You CAN'T See (We Shrink Down Things To Ant Size So Criminals Can't Steal Them, So That's Why That Capitalization Makes Sense)

Brain Drain is not a trained pilot, which is why he's ejecting instead of trying to land that jet. I thought about it and it's exactly what I'd do in that situation, which means it is extremely realistic, because I myself am also extremely realistic!!

Scott's just lucky that Maureen left all the cod, fiddle music, poutine, and dulse inside.

There are some international borders that go right through the middle of cities, even buildings! Borders are *crazy!* Nobody tell Brain Drain though, it sounds like he's got enough opinions about them already.

That Canadian human-powered pleasure craft law is legit. Also, yes, Canadian lawyers call canoes "human-powered pleasure craft," which should tell you all you need to know about Canadian lawyers.

en my dog cries I ask him about his big important feelings, and he never replies, possibly because it's *really hard* to say "your big important feelings" and still sound sincere.

Whoa, this was *not* part of the Ant-Plan!!

Anyway, OFF we go to America! While we ***could*** easily look behind ourselves right now, we all know there's nothing but an empty island there, so it's definitely not worth our time. Onward, friends!!

Look, I'm not saying ants are organizing themselves into a world-spanning superorganism. I'm just saying that when they *do*, y'all have no excuse for acting surprised.

...then we definitely have a chance.
WELCOME TO TORONTO
EXIT:
ENIGMO
GARDINER
EXPRESSWAY 3km
Traffic team to police: We have unauthorized movement on the Enigmo Expressway.
Acknowledged. Intercepting.
And they definitely don't have a chance.
WEE-OO-WEE-OO-W
Again, to reiterate, I sincerely feel like we have a definite chance against Enigmo here, assuming of course that we can reach NYC, which, again, I have no reason to expect that we won't.
...Hey, anyone else hear that??

Does Ant-Man always make a "PWEEOOP" sound effect when he shrinks, and if he doesn't, why does he *refuse* to live his best life??

Here Lies Ant-Van, 1975-2016. Beloved Friend of the Kra-Van, the Stilt-Van, and the Iron Van. She Will Be Missed.

See?? All we're missing is the One Twitchy Person Who Says They're Fine To Pull OFF A Heist, But You Just Know They're So Not Fine To Pull OFF A Heist, and we'll be *set!*

Our mistake was trying to take Enigmo head-on. You don't fight a guy you can't punch.
Right. Right.
He can beat you in a fight, so obviously you don't fight him. You heist him instead.
And you steal freedom back.
Oh, Doreen, now you're speaking my language.
SCHLOORP
...And mine too, Scott.
Next month: Catharsis! Escalating action!
Finding out why this one Engimo has been stalking our gang! AND MORE??

Dear Squirrel Girl Crew,

Issue 11 was a triumph. I loved the numerical puzzles and the scene with Doreen caught in a final exam nightmare really hit home. I have a variation of her dream from time to time. There's a class I haven't attended and need to drop to avoid a failing grade. Trouble is, I can never find the building I need to go to in order to drop the class (and Nightmare is probably cursing himself for not adding that Kafkaesque touch for Squirrel Girl).

There was a little note on fan fiction. I just did a bit of that, if you are interested. In my previous letter, I said I'd like to see Squirrel Girl take on the White Rabbit. Via Amazon, I was able to buy the Rabbit's first appearance, Marvel Team Up 131. I did a customer review there, imagining the White Rabbit asking Marvel editors about the state of her career (she was not happy).

Sincerely,
Robert Fisher

RYAN: I saw a lot of people saying "HEY, I HAD THAT RECURRING DREAM TOO!" not realizing that it's pretty common. It's really common, turns out! Though not being able to find the building is a good twist. I'd tell dream-you to try doing it on your phone, I guess?

I am BIG INTO this fan fiction, and also, I am BIG INTO nobody correcting me on the error in #11! Thank you all for that. In case you missed it, there was a point where Doreen said that by using binary you can count to 1031 on both hands. If you tried it, you'll see this is incorrect: you actually only get to 1023! I'm not even gonna blame Doreen for this one: it was my fault! I just typed in the wrong number. But I wanted to mention it here, in case anyone got into "who can count the highest on their hands" competitions and then got stuck because of my mistake. Let this error happen... NO LONGER!!

ERICA: I've never dropped a class, so the version of the dream that I have is that I realize by mid term or finals that there's a class I never attended and I need to get there to try to make a last ditch effort to pass it but I don't know where it is or how to find the office that could help me (by this point the school has become a labyrinth).

Dear Unbeatable Squirrel-friends,

I AM SO HAPPY! Both the writing and art in this book just brightens my day every time it shows up in my pull-box! The writing is clever and these little human moments give me life. And Erica's designs and panel composition match perfectly to really make SG Stand out from the other hero books out there!

I was so excited to meet Ryan at Zdarscon this year too, hopefully next time Erica is in Toronto I get to gush to her too!

Squirrel girl is a fun, totally rad character and thanks to you guys she keeps showing up in more places! Every time I show her to my friends they fall in love.

I hope she joins in on the fun for Monsters Unleashed! The whole concept seems to be made just for her!

Yes we Pecan,
Jakob Withakay

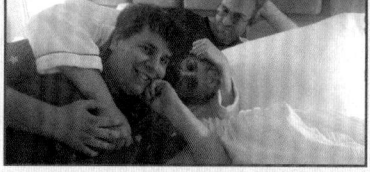

RYAN: Haha, so, I feel like "Chip Zdarsky Presents: Zdarscon" (pictured above in Jakob's photo) needs some explanation? But then I also feel like it works just as well if you have no idea what's going on! So, BASICALLY Chip (the same Chip from HOWARD THE DUCK! We did a crossover once! What a guy!) rented a hotel room and had his own mini convention in Toronto, and he invited me and a bunch of other friends to come greet fans and readers! He wore a bathrobe all day because it's his hotel room and who is gonna tell him what to do, and I wore my Star Trek pajamas because I will take any excuse to wear my Star Trek pajamas (Engineering division).

ERICA: SO. The last time I saw Ryan was the day after the Eisner award ceremony (WHERE WE WERE UP FOR TWO EISNERS *COUGH*). We were getting lunch and he tells me about these Star Trek pajamas and asks if he should buy them. I probably said something along the lines of "It's your money" and warned him that most pajamas aren't made for men who are 6'6". ANYWAY my point is that the moment they started posting photos from Zdarscon all I could think was "oh my god he did it. How do those fit on him?" That is Erica's story from home, 1 hour away (by plane) from Zdarscon. My fiance did ask if I wanted to go to Zdarscon but CHIP NEVER ASKED ME TO. I see how it is, Zdarsky. I see how it is.

Hi Ryan and Erica,

I just finished issue 11 – hilarious as usual! At first I was sorry to see Erica had a fill-in artist, but was blown away by Jacob's work. Any time you need a vacation Erica, please request Jacob to step in again. (Or was it even a vacation? I have a sneaking suspicion someone was working on what is sure to be my new favorite original graphic novel. Wink wink!)

So, I had to write in and share a squirrel sighting with you all. I was hiking with a buddy on Assateague Island off of Virginia's Eastern Shore and was proselytizing about USG and how he needed to read it. Lo and behold, we crossed paths with the Delmarva Fox Squirrel. I wish I had gotten a pic, but alas I did not. I don't think a photo would have done the animal justice though. In pictures it looks like a lighter-colored grey squirrel, but in person it really does look like a fox except it moves in the herky-jerky way that squirrels do. And it was quite a bit bigger than a grey squirrel to boot!

Keep up the great work. Looking forward to Unbeatable Squirrel Girl Beats Up the Marvel Universe! Cheers,

Charles Albert
Richmond, VA

RYAN: Delmarva Fox Squirrel! Awesome. You probably know this, but for everyone else: DID YOU KNOW that the Delmarva Fox Squirrel used to be on the endangered species list? But they're off it now! We got them off the list by not destroying their habitat quite as much (always a good idea if you want to help), and by reintroducing them to new areas that we thought they'd do well in. They were added to the list in 1967 and they were taken off the list just a few months ago, in November 2015! Another neat thing about these squirrels is they don't hop from tree to tree, but rather climb down one tree, travel across the ground, and then climb up the next one. Safety first!

ERICA: Jacob is great. I'm so glad that I was able to get him. I had A WEEKEND to find a fill-in. Yeah, that month was basically the opposite of a vacation.

Squirrels I hope to see in real life: Malabar Giant Squirrel, Japanese Dwarf Flying Squirrel, Jill the famous instagram squirrel, Theo the also famous instagram squirrel.

Dear Ryan & Erica,

I used to collect comics when I was younger, but I stopped about ten years ago. I've gotten back into them this year, and series like yours are the reason why. As far as I'm concerned, THE UNBEATABLE SQUIRREL GIRL is the best, most consistently high-quality book being published right now. I would go so far as to say it's the best comic of the last decade (at ast)! Given how good it is, I couldn't keep it o myself. I've gotten my boyfriend into comics oo, and Squirrel Girl is his absolute favorite.

Much love and admiration,
Eric (and Trevor)

P.S. Is there any chance that Doreen's old eammates from the GLA will ever show up for n issue? Also, I hope we haven't seen the last f that Sentinel Doreen dated!

RYAN: Eric, Trevor: thank you for these uper kind words! I'm really glad you and our boyfriend like our talking squirrel omics. Hooray! As for the GLA – there's a ew GREAT LAKES AVENGERS comic coming ut soon! It's written by your friend and nine Zac Gorman, with art by Will Robson. t looks REALLY GREAT. As for the Sentinel, think about him often and hope he's doing vell.

ERICA: I think Doreen would say that they veren't dating, they just went on one date.

Dear Ryan and Erica,
I enjoyed the binary nightmare, but one opic strikes me, Doreen's diet doesn't seem o have a hazelnut in every bite. What is this alafel fascination? Are Doreen and Nancy ixated on grass? Or don't they know how to ook beans-on-toast or Marmite spaghetti like ormal students? They will get rickets!

Isn't there a Spidey Student Survival book vith Aunt May's wheatcake recipe? Or does Katie Morag need to spill the beans on how o make a poridggy? We need a sign on how Squirrel Girl gets her five day, if she is going to emain a beacon of clean living.

Now that Doreen has taught the world to ount, she needs to teach the world to cook, or uy it a Coke, which ever is easier.

Yours sincerely,

Simon Rogers,
United Kingdom

PS Surely Mr and Mrs Nefaria were Count nd Countess Nefaria, unless the current Count ought the title from one of those companies hat sell plots of land on the Moon or surface of the Sun?

RYAN: Simon, I would not put it past the Count to get suckered by one of those scams. As for Doreen's diet, I would actually really ike to know Aunt May's wheatcake recipe. There WAS a Marvel cookbook years ago called "Stan Lee Presents: The Mighty Marvel Superheroes' Cookbook," because of course it was) but it was published in 1977 and includes recipes like "Spidey's Chocolate Web Pancakes" which tells you o "prepare pancakes according to the instructions on the package," put them n a stack, and then "form a web by criss-crossing lines with liquid chocolate syrup across the top." There's also a recipe for "easy raisin bread" that is just "take pre-sliced bread, push raisins into bread." In conclusion, I hope you enjoyed these two delicious recipes.

ERICA: I'm not going to lie, I don't know what y'all are talking about because I have been so busy that I never got around to reading issue 11! I still don't know how to use my fingers to count in binary! I'm just going to talk generally about food then. As a vegetarian, Doreen would have to be fairly conscious of her diet since her lifestyle more or less requires her to eat like a mini Dwayne "The Rock" Johnson but without depleting the oceans of cod. In this case falafel isn't a bad choice since beans and legumes are an excellent source of protein, something you're going to need if you're lifting cars on a regular basis. Nuts are also a great source of healthy fat and bursts of energy. Fun fact: Squirrels can't eat just nuts because they'll get too fat. They crave nuts because getting fat is good for the winter but they also need fungi, greens, fruits and insects. That's right! Squirrels are omnivores! They'll also eat snakes, other rodents and birds. So Doreen's vegetarianism is less about being like a squirrel and more about realizing that animals are sentient. I don't think that answered any questions you might have had but it's been so long I don't remember what they might have been.

Dear Ryan and Erica,
On Sept. 3, 2016, Squirrel Girl taught me how to count to 31 on one hand. Coincidentally, Sept. 3, 2016, was my 31st birthday. So, now, I am this many. Thanks Doreen.

Mike LaRowe (a.k.a. the Semi-Beatable Man Boy) in Grand Rapids (a.k.a. Beer City USA (for real))

RYAN: HAPPY BELATED BIRTHDAY, MIKE!! If we meet I'll give you a high five, or rather... a high thirty-one?

Dear Squirrely Duo,
I loved the Computer Science themed issue. Doreen knows the Powers of Two!

More CS fun:

```
if (you dare to pick a fight with Doctor Octopus) {
    you have sealed your fate
    for (i do not forgive) {
        i do not give up on revenge
    }
}
```

Since the 'for' loop has no exit condition, it will run forever: "I do not give up..."

You left that as an easter egg for us, didn't you? Admit it!

I used to have the exam nightmare. But once, it was --math--. Looking at the first question, I could see what it was driving at. Even though I hadn't taken the course, I was able to derive the answer from what I already knew. Same with the second question. It was like being invited to explore a new mathematical domain, step by step. It felt wonderful! I turned in my paper knowing I had aced the test.

I haven't had that nightmare since.

Beat up the Marvel Universe? I'm only following two Marvel titles at the moment.

I'd like to see the Unbeatable Squirrel Girl kick back with the Unbelievable Gwenpool over pizza and sodas.

Very mostly yours,
John Prenis

RYAN: Man that sounds like THE MOST SATISFYING NIGHTMARE EVER IN TIME. I love it. I used to have Doreen's nightmare too, but I solved it like she did – talking to the Dean – and I haven't really had it since. But I barely EVER remember my dreams or nightmares, so it's actually kinda nice to have a nightmare and wake up, because then at least I get to remember my dreams!

I have friends who have dreams that tell actual STORIES, and then when they wake up they can lift their dreams for stories they're working on, and I'm really jealous. They're literally getting work done in their sleep! MUST BE NICE.

ERICA: For a while I had episodic continuing dreams about having to stop an apocalyptic cult. Maybe we can use that? That sounds like our sort of thing. Marvel HAS A DUDE NAMED APOCALYPSE.

Next Issue:

Attention, Squirrel Scouts! Make sure to check out our production blog, **unbeatablesquirrelgirl.tumblr.com**, where we post behind-the-scenes stuff on how the book gets made, along with all sorts of cool things *you* make: fanart, cosplay, whatever!

The unbeatable Squirrel Girl

Doreen Green isn't just a second-year computer science student: she secretly also has all the powers of both squirrel and girl! She uses her amazing abilities to fight crime **and** be as awesome as possible. You know her as...**The Unbeatable Squirrel Girl!** Find out what she's been up to, with...

Squirrel Girl *in a nutshell*

Squirrel Girl @unbeatablesg
Hey everyone guess who's back from her vacation in Northern Canada where she couldn't get a cell signal?

Squirrel Girl @unbeatablesg
And now she's in SOUTHERN Canada where she can easily get a cell signal, only this dude named Enigmo has taken over??

Squirrel Girl @unbeatablesg
And so now she's gotta deal with THAT baloney RIGHT AWAY even though she never got more than a few pages into Lake Enthusiast Magazine???

Squirrel Girl @unbeatablesg
Anyway yeah it's me. HELLO ENIGMO YOU SHUT DOWN SMS MESSAGING BUT WE CAN STILL HANG OUT HERE ON SOCIAL MEDIA

Squirrel Girl @unbeatablesg
anyway send me your freshest anti-Enigmo memes, as far as we know that could be his only weakness so it's good to be prepared I guess

Egg @imduderadtude
@unbeatablesg omg ive waited my whole life for this moment

Tony Stark @starkmantony
@unbeatablesg Good to have you back. We, uh, haven't had much luck defeating this guy in NYC. He splits apart into other guys.

Squirrel Girl @unbeatablesg
@starkmantony Not a problem, Tony!! I once beat a guy made of a bunch of bees who could split apart into regular bees! NO BIG DEAL.

Tony Stark @starkmantony
@unbeatablesg I can use this. What'd you do?

Squirrel Girl @unbeatablesg
@starkmantony Oh, bees can't fly when they're wet so I got him wet and then took bags of wet bees to the police. ANOTHER CRIME WELL FOUGHT

Tony Stark @starkmantony
@unbeatablesg This...helps me precisely 0%.

Squirrel Girl @unbeatablesg
@starkmantony I'm on it, dude!! Me and Ant-Man came up with a plan to save everything! I can't tell you it publicly but let me just say

Squirrel Girl @unbeatablesg
@starkmantony WE ARE GONNA HEIST FREEDOM BACK

Squirrel Girl @unbeatablesg
@starkmantony ME and TIPPY and ANT-MAN and BRAIN DRAIN and MY MOM and MY GOOD FRIEND are gonna HEIST FREEDOM BACK

Squirrel Girl @unbeatablesg
@starkmantony AND IT'S DEFINITELY GONNA WORK

Squirrel Girl @unbeatablesg
@starkmantony AND WE'RE GONNA GO DO IT RIGHT NOW SO WHEN YOU NEXT HEAR FROM ME IT'LL BE ME SAYING "GLAD MY PLAN WENT PERFECTLY, LOL"

Squirrel Girl @unbeatablesg
@starkmantony I'm not sure if I'll say "lol" or not yet though

Tony Stark @starkmantony
@unbeatablesg Yeah you always gotta play that by ear lol

Squirrel Girl @unbeatablesg
@starkmantony Tony

Squirrel Girl @unbeatablesg
@starkmantony It's weird when you do it

search!

- #toronto
- #cityhall
- #heistmusic
- #parentalleave
- #physics

When we last saw Squirrel Girl, she had come up with a plan to HEIST FREEDOM BACK. Let's see how that worked out!
Dang it! How did our plan fail so completely?! How does this even happen??
AS YOU WILL RECALL WE HAD JUST ESCAPED ENIGMO BY SHRINKING, BUT THEN WERE QUICKLY SPOTTED BY ANOTHER ENIGMO
WHICH ONLY ILLUSTRATES THE ESSENTIAL AND MADDENING FUTILITY OF OUR UNIVERSE
33

OF *course* there's an Empire State University course on nihilism. OF *course* Nancy took that as her mandatory English elective.

"Here's the deal: years ago I was a star in the *Unlimited Class Wrestling Federation.* Remember them? Everyone in the league had powers.

"But *somehow,* people got tired of watching a rock man fight a man who can become tinier men. Sales dropped, and the league closed.

"And just like that, I was homeless.

"I was stolen from, beaten up, attacked. People looked at me with everything from cold indifference to actual hatred.

"I saw humanity at its worst.

ANYTHING HELPS

"One day I was attacked by someone who wanted what little money I had. But when we all rejoined to fight our attacker...

Aah, my nose!

"...I didn't.

"I watched myself fight back. I watched myself get hurt. And then I watched myself leave.

"And that was it. I decided I'd had enough of people for a while. I lived off the grid. Eventually snuck into Canada.

"And that's where I ran into you, on my little island."

That island thing happened in *The Unbeatable Squirrel Girl #13,* which came out directly before this issue! Come on, man! *SERIAL STORYTELLING WORKS BEST IF YOU READ THE ISSUES IN ORDER, WE'RE TRYING HARD HERE BUT YOU GOTTA HELP US OUT AT LEAST A LITTLE!!*

Can you tell an Ant-Man story and *not* have a heist in it? It is a question science is unable to answer, because the second someone tries, they're like, "Man, what if I just put a fun heist in here though??"

HEIST-PLANNING MONTAGE SEQUENCE

Play cool heist-planning music while reading this page for full effect.

See? *Brain Drain* played *his* heist-planning music. I can only assume you did the same. (For what it's worth, his song was *"Planning Our Heist (Wow That's Nice)"* by Sir Heist-A-Lot And His Three Pals Who Aren't That Into The Concepts Of Property Or Personal Ownership.)

I JUST ASSUMED YOU WERE TALKING ABOUT SOME OTHER WISE ELDER HEISTMASTER! I DUNNO, MAYBE MY MOM?

America, I don't think having a baby is as cheap or as easy as your social safety net would seem to imply!!
SORRY, AMERICA, BUT BABIES EAT, LIKE, 100% OF THE TIME THEY AREN'T SLEEPING OR CRYING.

Making the good Enigmo look different was definitely not done just because it makes the good Enigmo easy to identify for you, the reader, when he shows up four pages from now. It *also* lets us draw and write about cool hats!!

Uh, clearly that guy does, Ant-Man. It's *right there*. Also, that's not the good Enigmo! *His* ball cap is red and has a maple leaf on it. We almost tricked you, huh??

I've got a note here from Deadpool from the last issue. It reads as follows: "CALLED IT."

Nancy and Squirrel Girl both know what that square-cube law is, but do you? Naw, me neither. But instead of throwing this comic away in a fit of ***incandescent rage,*** let's all keep in mind that there's a small chance this might be explained on the very next page!

This is actual physics, and Galileo actually did discover this! It was during what I can only assume was an ahead-of-his-time attempt to invent an enlarging ray, before he eFocused on just, you know, astronomy, math, engineering, physics, science, and philosophy. *Also yes, that is the good Enigmo there in the last panel, you found him.*

Action Figures not pictured include: "Hellcat (But in Canadian Clothes)," "Howard the Canadian Duck (So I Guess That Means He's A Northern Shoveler Duck Or Something)," and "Angela: Queen of Halifax."

And so...
--and that concludes my detailed explanation of our new plan/semi-improvised theater which we're about to put into action. Everyone on board?
I'm gonna need a minute to make the modifications.
CITY HALL PARKING GARAGE
You've got 30 seconds, Scott!! Enigmo's gonna notice that we're not actually in the middle of that giant fight scene real quick. Just do your best!
If I die, I want my gravestone to read "Here lies Scott Lang, he died as he lived: knowing that Squirrel Girl's plan was megabad all along."
Man, nobody's dying or getting funny gravestones today!! Move out!
15 seconds later...
Enigmos! Your attention, please!
I just want y'all to know, I didn't want to have to do this!
I'd hoped for a peaceful resolution to this conflict. But it looks like that's not gonna happen today. So instead I guess I'm gonna just have to blast you all to smithereens.
Don't know what to tell you, dudes! Should've listened when you heard I was unbeatable!!
You don't even have any blasters!! What are you gonna do?
Oh, Bad Enigmos...
JUST WATCH ME.

Not necessarily giant mechas, but giant mechas if necessary.

We've got the right idea! Everyone: emergency merge!
We're gonna merge bigger than we've ever merged before!
SCHLOORP SCHLOORP
Destroy the mecha! Wrestle it to the ground!
SCHLOORP SCHLOORP SCHLOORP
That's right, Canadians do apologize all the time! But it's not because we accidentally bumped into you on the sidewalk. Oh no.
Those were preemptive apologies. For what we knew we'd one day have to do. For what we're about to do...
...right now.
I'd say that's our cue.
Engaging "Repulsor Blast Action With Sound Effects!!"

Eat Canadian mecha Iron Man repulsor rays, jerks!!
PUEEEEEEE
You're going down, Squirrel Girl!!
KRAAK

OWWWW!!
Enigmo! Brain Drain! Tippy!
Enigmo's falling! Get out of the way!!
GOOD ENIGMO, WE HAVE BEEN TOLD TO ESCAPE THE FALLING GIANT. INSTEAD YOU CHOOSE TO RUN TOWARDS OBLIVION, WHICH WE AS A PEOPLE HAVE DECIDED IS SOMETHING YOU'RE NOT SUPPOSED TO DO
FOR SOME REASON
Go, go!! I'm not gonna get crushed! The force of this weight will be enough to merge me! I know it!!
SCHLOO--
I can save us! Me and my brothers working together!! I can do this!
--OORP
THUD
I BELIEVE THIS PROVES THREE THINGS:
1) THAT GOOD ENIGMO WAS ON OUR SIDE AFTER ALL
2) THAT SOMETIMES THIS INDIFFERENT WORLD CAN STILL OFFER UP A SURPRISING MOMENT OF GRACE
AND THE FINAL THING IT PROVES, TIPPY, IS 3) BODIES ARE GROSS AND NOBODY SHOULD GET ONE UNDER ANY CIRCUMSTANCES
Chhht!

Did you know: Toronto's actual slogan is "Diversity Our Strength"? I only realized that halfway through writing this story! And now you've got one more "Fun Canada Fact" in your brain, PLUS a bonus "Semi-boring Ryan Fact" too!

SQUIRREL GIRL, NANCY, TIPPY, AND MAUREEN FINISHED THEIR VACATION IN NOVA SCOTIA, FAMOUS FOR ITS FIDDLE MUSIC, STRIKING NATURAL BEAUTY, ACADIAN CULTURE...AND REMARKABLY FEW SUPER VILLAINS.
CANADA
TO ANT-MAN
THE CANADIAN GOVERNMENT GAVE ANT-MAN A BONUS FOR NOT SMASHING UP THE ENTIRE CITY HALL WHILE SAVING IT, WHICH HAPPENED, TO BE FOR THE PRECISE AMOUNT ANT-MAN OWED FOR HIS LOST PLANE, SO THAT WAS NICE.
SCOTT'S ROLE IN SAVING THE WORLD GOT HIS BUSINESS A LOT OF ATTENTION...
...ENOUGH TO EASILY AFFORD A REPLACEMENT ANT-VAN.
BRAIN DRAIN CONTINUED TO FIGHT CRIME AND HIS OWN ENNUI IN NYC...
...BUT NOW IN A NEW COSTUME MADE FOR HIM BY MAUREEN.
ENIGMO DENOUNCED TRYING TO REPLACE HUMANITY WITH HIMSELF, AND INSTEAD, 14% OF HIS TOTAL BIOMASS PURSUED A MASTERS DEGREE IN THEORETICAL PHYSICS.
SCIENCE EVENTUALLY RECOVERED FROM BEING ABUSED BY BOTH PYM PARTICLES AND COSMIC RAYS, AND CONTINUES TO BE THE BEST WAY TO EXPLORE THE WORKINGS OF OUR UNIVERSE.
THE (REAL, FINAL) END.

You folks get many letters from young girls in whose lives you have been important, which is great. I am not a small girl. I am a guy who is approaching 50. Squirrel Girl is very important to my life.

For the last few years, I have been dealing with chronic pain, unemployment, and (unsurprisingly) depression. The Unbeatable Squirrel Girl has made me *literally* laugh out loud a bare minimum of once every single issue, often more. (Most recently with "So I cannot give it my full recommendation.") Laughs can be hard to come by. You deliver.

No pressure,
Alexx

RYAN: Alexx, thank you so much. That's what we're here for! I've got a friend with chronic pain and it is such a daily struggle, so to have unemployment and depression on top of that -- it's rough, dude. I know what we do is small in the grand scheme of things, but I'm really happy that we can help you out, even a little!

ERICA: I think one of the things that has surprised me the most is the range of people who have told me they enjoy the book. I'm really glad that we could make something that has positively affected your life.

Ryan and Erica:

Your mention of Koi Boi heading off to visit the ruins of the underwater kingdom of New Atlantis brought a couple of questions to mind:

1) Will you be presenting that as a Squirrel Girl special episode? There are usually technology raiders searching out hidden Atlantean technology in their ruins (not to mention trying to find Atlantean skeletons to sell on the alternative medicine black market). Surely Koi Boi is likely to run into one of them. If not, a guided Visitors' Board tour of the ruins might be quite beautiful. Unfortunately, I can't remember which destruction of Atlantis this ruin is from. Was it bombed, nuked, or biologically destroyed? Hmm, why was Koi Boi going there again?

2) Koi are fresh water fish. New Atlantis is in salt water. I seem to remember Koi Boi swimming in the harbor area so I assume that he can breathe heavily polluted salt water but can he also breathe fresh water? Does his amphibious nature allow him to breathe both? Does he have to use special breathing equipment in one water or the other? Did Tony Stark make the salt filter / infuser unit for him? Man, this would make a really interesting Biology 201 class at his college!

Thanks for an entertaining comic,
Geoffrey Tolle
Lord of Squirrels (as soon as I start my 40 generation domestication project).

RYAN: 1) I don't think we'll show it! Normally I'd say "use your imagination," but you have clearly already done this, so I guess all I can say is "thanks for using your imagination!" If you could fill out that plot to 20 pages and send over a script, I'd be happy to take the credit for it!!

2) I think Erica and I discussed this and we agreed Koi Boi could breathe both salt and fresh water, but I admit we did not work out the specifics! Although MAYBE the fact that the original Atlantis is in fresh water is the reason everyone's had such a hard time finding it! MAYBE??

ERICA: I'm pretty sure he's good in all types of water. He can talk to all the fish and really just had to pick one to go with for the name. "Fish Boy" just doesn't cut it, you know?

Guys, Atlantis was built on the ruins of the original Atlantis 8,000 years ago. Anything that was there from the Great Cataclysm is surely in an underwater museum or merged into the new construction (like Rome) by now.

Ryan and Erica,

Wow guys, this comic is just swell. Squirrel Girl is truly unbeatable, and Nancy is such a rad character, and Koi Boy and Chipmunk Hunk are undeniably the most perfectly named super heroes ever. And geez, Brain Drain is just trying so hard to be a good superhero and I just...I just want him to be happy. I love you, Brain Drain, and I will always be proud of you. No matter what.

Squirrelfully Yours,

Elisha Smith
Knoxville, TN

RYAN: Aw, thank you! I -- I really love Brain Drain too. I am surprised at how cute he is, and I love how Erica has turned a literal brain with a pair of eyes attached into somehow the most facially expressive character. SHE IS MAGIC.

ERICA: I love our crazy nihilist brain trapped in a robot body trying to be a superhero.

Dear Letters From Nuts,

I wanted to draw attention to an apparent discrepancy on the cover of issue #11. There the binary numbering is displayed in six digits, 001011, whereas five digits, 01011 would seem more applicable, since Doreen teaches Count Nefaria (and us readers) how to count in binary on a single hand, and five fingers equal five digits. Sidenote: the English word "digit" comes from the Latin word for "finger" -- how appropriate!

At first, I thought the cover numbering might have something to do with squirrels having six fingers, but a hasty Google image search revealed that four front fingers and five hind fingers are the usual sciurine characteristics. I flipped through the issue again and found no evidence of polydactyly.

Then it dawned on me: the six-digit binary numbering must have come from Doctor Octopus, who is right there on the cover. Raising one arm and the two opposite tentacles while keeping his other three not-being-used-for-standing appendages lowered is naturally how Doc Ock would flash his digits!

Does this explanation entitle me to a No-Prize? I do hope so! I've long aspired to the rank of Titanic True Believer (T.T.B.), which would in turn bump me up to Permanent Marvelite Maximus (P.M.M.).

Best,
Morris Tichenor, R.F.O., Q.N.S., K.O.F.
Toronto, ON

P.S. More etymology fun: the Latin word "digitus" probably derives from "dico" (meaning "to speak" + the suffix "-itus"). I like to image Romans gesticulated wildly whenever they spoke.

P.P.S. I want to second Erica's assertion that Nomad's Lorenzo Lamas phase is "the BEST Nomad." Thanks for giving a shout-out to one of my favorite '90s titles.

RYAN: Man I love a letter that starts out with "HERE IS A PROBLEM" and ends with "NEVERMIND, I HAVE COME UP WITH A SOLUTION TO THE PROBLEM THAT ONLY

EQUIRES YOU PRETEND THAT YOU WERE MARTER THAN YOU ACTUALLY ARE," hich is something I am more than willing do and may actually already be doing. is my understanding that No-Prizes are r THIS VERY THING, which makes me xtremely excited about No-Prizes. My nderstanding that they're just pictures f empty envelopes makes me LESS xcited, but, well, here we are. (Also the added zeroes worked nicely from a design erspective, so really, TWO good reasons o do it that way.) ENJOY THE PRIZE:

ERICA: I... still haven't read #11, but hat's important is that the issue you're urrently reading got to the printers by the eadline.

I'm really hoping that now that Steve s on the run in the Marvel Cinematic U, e're going to get at least a moment of him ith his hair grown out riding a motorcycle round. I know that he wasn't Nomad uring that time, but we have to work with vhat we're given. Also, we know he can ide a motorcycle.

ear Squirrel Girl Crew:

I enjoyed Squirrel Girl's run-in with the ole Man. It looks like next month, we an expect Dr. Octopus and Venom. While quirrel Girl certainly has taken on some of Marvel's big name villains, I recently became nterested in one of the lesser lights. Might I uggest that Squirrel Girl versus the legend-n-her-own-mind White Rabbit would have ome great possibilities?

Sincerely
Robert Fisher

RYAN: The time delay on these letters neans you have already (hopefully!) read he comic and seen what happens! Doc Ock nd Venom are two of my favorite bad guys, o it was a treat to put them both in the same ssue (KINDA, AGAIN, I CAN ONLY ASSUME OU READ IT BUT DON'T WANT TO SPOIL NYTHING). In any case, to answer your uestion, I just looked up the White Rabbit nd she has a giant robot rabbit that fires nissiles, so I'm already totally down with er whole thing.

ERICA: If you've read this issue, it robably means you just finished a three-ssue arc starring a character who has only een in TWO OTHER ISSUES IN ALL OF ARVEL'S 70+ YEAR HISTORY. We're into he deep cuts too, is all I'm sayin'. I feel ike one of the hardest parts of doing this s picking who the villain will be each time. Ve're literally going through that right now lanning for issue #17. I feel like this is ne one thing we have trouble agreeing on ometimes.

Another cracker from Ryan and Erica - kicking off with Spider-Man getting in on the Twitter conversation - and who is he kidding when he says that his webshooters make that "thwip" sound? We know that just like Wolverine, he makes that noise himself.

Count Nefaria was wonderful and the footnotes were right, we were all doing the counting on our fingers too. Very elegant solution to the nightmare about exams, which we've all had.

There are lots of good comics about at the moment, but Squirrel Girl, each and every issue is just a JOY. Easily the nicest lead character around - and isn't it lovely to show that you don't have to be dark or angsty or driven to be a compelling lead - you can actually be kind and perky too.

(Jacob - the facial expression on Count Nefaria's face in the "no way, you've got to teach me" panel was just perfect)

Many thanks

Andrew Pack
Brighton, England

RYAN: Yeah, Jacob did a terrific job on that issue, and I loved that we got to show that Doreen's dreams are a little brighter than the real world. That seems to fit, you know? Thank you for all these kind words, and I can only hope that future authors continue to characterize Count Nefaria as "a Dracula who likes numbers." IT WORKS, YO.

ERICA: I was so glad we got Jacob. I went to Wil with two names for who I'd like to use and Jacob wasn't even sure he could do it at the time, but we diiiiid iiiiit.

Dear Ryan, Erica, & Rico,

I first started reading Unbeatable Squirrel Girl after seeing a copy of the 1st volume at my library and thinking, "well, this looks ridiculous but potentially fun." Turns out it wasn't ridiculous (ok, maybe a little bit, but absolutely in a good way), and was more than just fun. I've been hooked on the adventures of Doreen, Tippy-Toe, & co. ever since. So much so that I cosplayed as Squirrel Girl for NYCC this year, and actually got to meet all of you (which was awesome)!

One of my favorite things about Squirrel Girl is that she doesn't just use the powers of squirrel, but those of girl as well. I love a good superhero fight scene, and Doreen can definitely kick butt (it's right there in her catchphrase) but my favorite moments are the ones where she uses reason, friendship, and sometimes even computer science to save the day. It's so refreshing to see a clever, optimistic, and ultimately inspiring superhero like Squirrel Girl who knows that it's often better to talk things out and solve problems with brains rather than fists.

Keep on eating nuts & kicking butts (and writing amazing new stories for Squirrel Girl)!

Rachel

P.S. I wish I could've gotten a photo with Rico too, but my friend had wandered off with the camera. Thank you so much for the button though, Rico! No one has asked me about my squirrel powers yet, but I remain hopeful.

RYAN: Rachel, it was SO GREAT to meet you at NYCC! At that show I was given my very own stuffed Tippy-Toe by a fan, so now I can pass as -- well, not Squirrel Girl, but Squirrel Earl at least. Your costume is amazing, and this letter is the best. I like the photo with Erica the best because it shows off your tail -- IT WAS A REALLY WELL-MADE TAIL, EVERYONE! Fun fact: NYCC was the first time Rico and I met in real life, and then later on we all went out to dinner and ate delicious guacamole. WE LIVED OUR BEST LIVES THAT DAY.

Next Issue:

Attention, Squirrel Scouts! Make sure to check out our production blog, **unbeatablesquirrelgirl.tumblr.com**, where we post behind-the-scenes stuff on how the book gets made, along with all sorts of cool things *you* make: fanart, cosplay, whatever!

the unbeatable Squirrel Girl
MEW
E.H.

Doreen Green isn't just a second-year computer science student: she secretly also has all the powers of both squirrel and girl! She uses her amazing abilities to fight crime **and** be as awesome as possible. You know her as...**The Unbeatable Squirrel Girl!** Find out what she's been up to, with...

Squirrel Girl *in a nutshell*

Nancy Whitehead @sewwiththeflo
zcadfewg5ttyniu,o;

Nancy Whitehead @sewwiththeflo
Hey everyone, sorry, my cat got on my keyboard and somehow posted that. Pretty cute though, right? Anyway, test post please ignore.

Nancy Whitehead @sewwiththeflo
';,l;joih87t67r5d4dsaqzdx

Nancy Whitehead @sewwiththeflo
Once more, sorry, Mew walked on my laptop again. Less cute the second time. I'll keep it closed from now on.

Nancy Whitehead @sewwiththeflo
hrzayus5f3iu6t54h76p8k70[k98;'--]\

Nancy Whitehead @sewwiththeflo
Okay okay she got on my phone this time but I PROMISE Mew will stop posting on my account.

Nancy Whitehead @sewwiththeflo
Thank you all for following me on social media today and I hoped you enjoyed this unscheduled #content.

Nancy Whitehead @sewwiththeflo
fmgnsjkbehrftyqu27334dfd5yn7c5jmikn,ob,lm;n9',

Nancy Whitehead @sewwiththeflo
Mew, how is this happening

Nancy Whitehead @sewwiththeflo
How is this happening, Mew

Nancy Whitehead @sewwiththeflo
XSCDV32CDN43KJ54HK6LUUMIK9OP97LKI

Nancy Whitehead @sewwiththeflo
Sorry, I'm sorry, I don't know how this keeps being a thing. I put my laptop under the bed WHILE LOGGED OUT, and yet here we are??

Nancy Whitehead @sewwiththeflo
VDSABCwvce32j43t56hy86jk98..l;jk

Nancy Whitehead @sewwiththeflo
Look all I can say is: if you followed me on this site then you knew the risks.

Squirrel Girl @unbeatablesg
@sewwiththeflo Maybe you should ask Mew to put her social media posts on... PAWS

Nancy Whitehead @sewwiththeflo
@unbeatablesg xacf435hy6gngj7ti7tj

Nancy Whitehead @sewwiththeflo
@unbeatablesg OKAY SHE'S REPLYING TO YOU NOW, HOLY COW, THIS IS CRAZY, WHAT IS GOING ON

Squirrel Girl @unbeatablesg
@sewwiththeflo I agree it's...CLAWS for concern

Nancy Whitehead @sewwiththeflo
@unbeatablesg I THINK I FIGURED IT OUT, YOU HAVE TO HIT CTRL+ENTER TO POST AND HER NATURAL GAIT REACHES THOSE TWO KEYS

Squirrel Girl @unbeatablesg
@sewwiththeflo but how is she getting the laptop open though??

Nancy Whitehead @sewwiththeflo
@unbeatablesg Listen, Mew is the best cat and therefore I'm sure she has her ways, but I'm CERTAIN now I've figured it out.

Nancy Whitehead @sewwiththeflo
@unbeatablesg It won't happen again. EVER.

Nancy Whitehead @sewwiththeflo
zwdreh4u7oi98p-['9=-=;p0lomnybtcdexweaq

Nancy Whitehead @sewwiththeflo
MEW

Nancy Whitehead @sewwiththeflo
WHY

Nancy Whitehead @sewwiththeflo
WHY, MEW

search!

#zcrg5ju7,i;

#lknmjguifte4w3q

#zcdvtnmukil;;;;;;;;;;

#8dfuetryt3#4

#cyuu6ui7jjmmm

SFFT
SFFT
SFFT
SOFT FOR THOR NOSES
DO NOT INGEST
Hey!
SNAK
Eugh. Good morning, Mew.
purrrrrr
Nancy get up
I'm up, I'm up.
Well good, because Taskmaster is invading the city and he's adapting to whatever gets thrown at him!!
So it's up to us to stop him, obviously!!
Sure is!
Ah. "Time to eat nuts and kick butts," I take it?
Don't get into any trouble, Mew.
purrrr
We'll have to get some more nuts on the way though, we're almost out.
They must love you at the bulk food store, Doreen.
GRAPESEED OIL
KLIK

the unbeatable Squirrel Girl
Presents:
THE MIGHTY MEWNIR
SMAK
purrrrr
DEADPOOL'S GUIDE TO SUPER VILLAINS
CARD 660 OF 4522
TASKMASTER
- THIS DUDE CAN "MASTER" ANY "TASK." JUST BY SEEING IT PERFORMED!
OH, THAT'S WHERE HIS NAME COMES FROM, HA HA I JUST REALIZED THAT, COOL
- IT'S SERIOUSLY CRAZY THOUGH, HE JUST HAS TO SEE SOMETHING AND HE
CAN DO IT PERFECTLY!! LIKE IF HE SEES AN OLYMPIC ATHLETE RAMP HER
BIKE OFF A SWEET JUMP, HE CAN INSTANTLY RAMP HIS OWN BIKE OFF A
SWEET JUMP EXACTLY AS WELL!!
- ANYWAY GUESS WHAT, THIS DUDE IS GREAT AT EVERYTHING AND YOU CAN'T
BEAT HIM IN A FIGHT BECAUSE HE CAN INSTANTLY MASTER YOUR OWN
SKILLS, AND THEN USE THEM AGAINST YOU.
THIS GUY CAN MASTER SOME FRIGGIN' TASKS, I'LL TELL YOU WHAT!
REALLY! AL MAN SHARK?? TO MIA OVIA OR ME "RUDE" OUT A D SHAME IN THE TIME ART SHARK.
OP MING AZY!!

SQUEAK SQUEAK
SNIKT
SNIKT
SQUEAK!!
SLLLIP
SMAK
SMAK
Sccreee!
SMAK
=sigh=

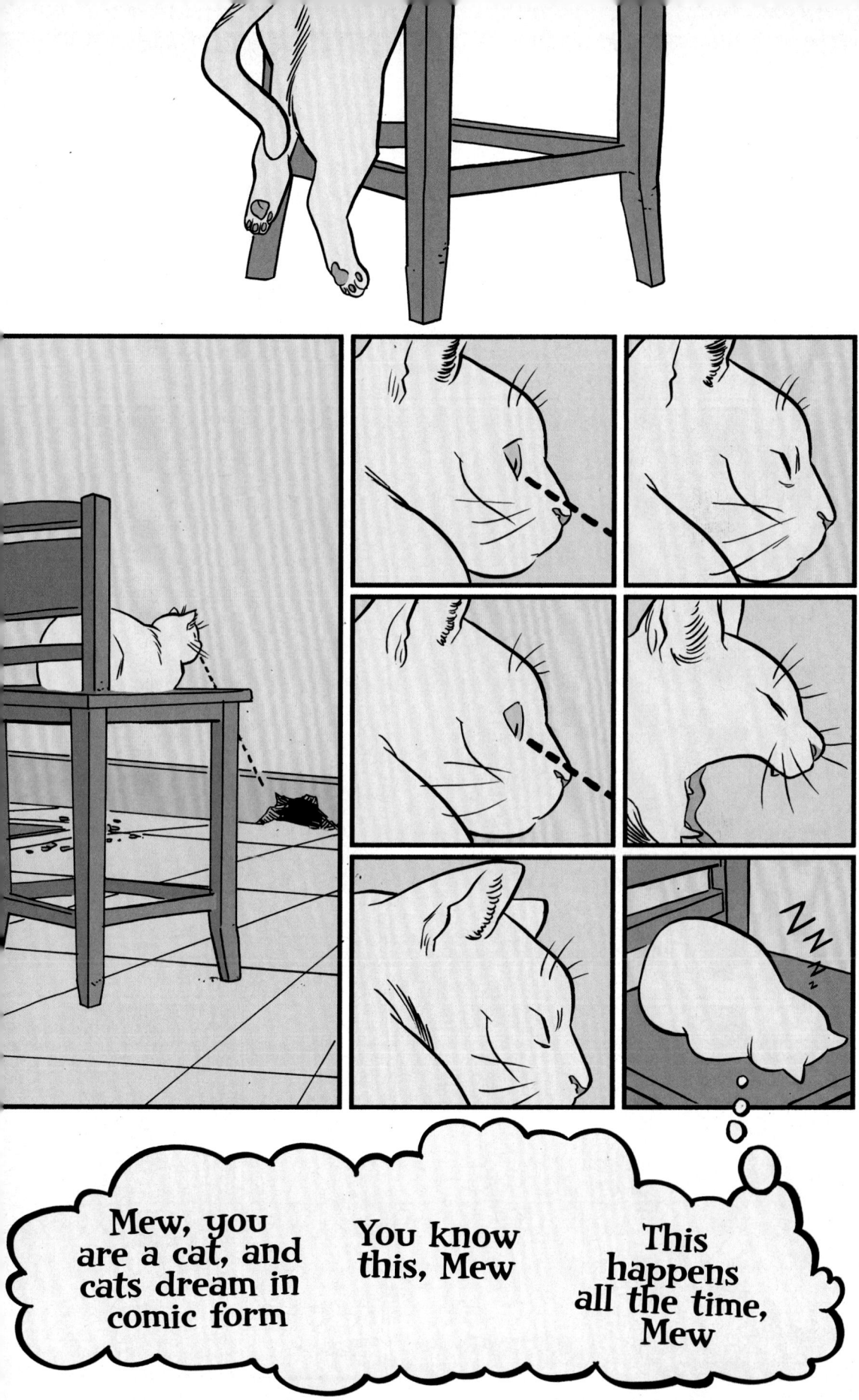
Mew, you are a cat, and cats dream in comic form
You know this, Mew
This happens all the time, Mew

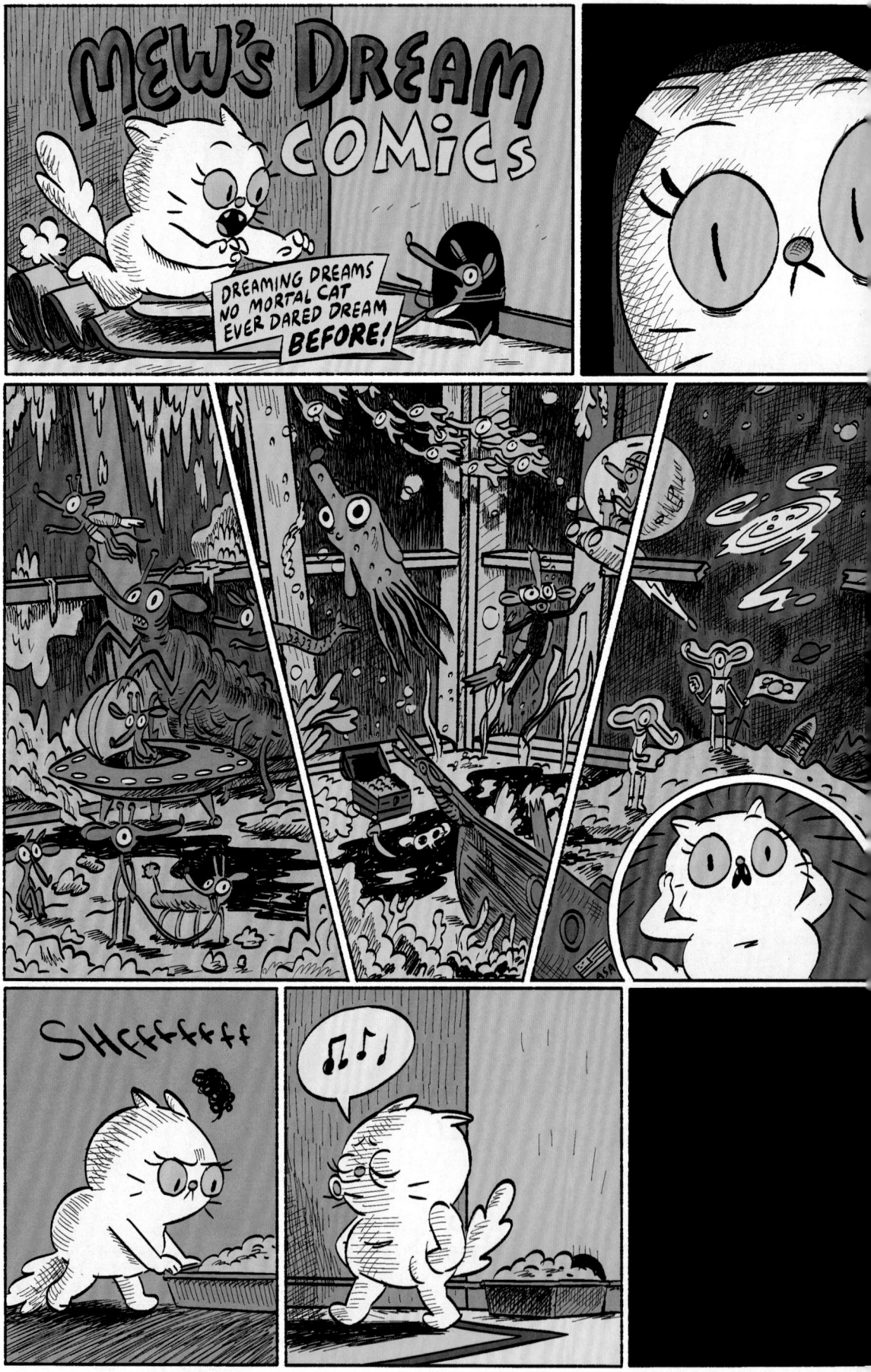
MEW'S DREAM COMICS
DREAMING DREAMS NO MORTAL CAT EVER DARED DREAM BEFORE!
SHFFFFFFF

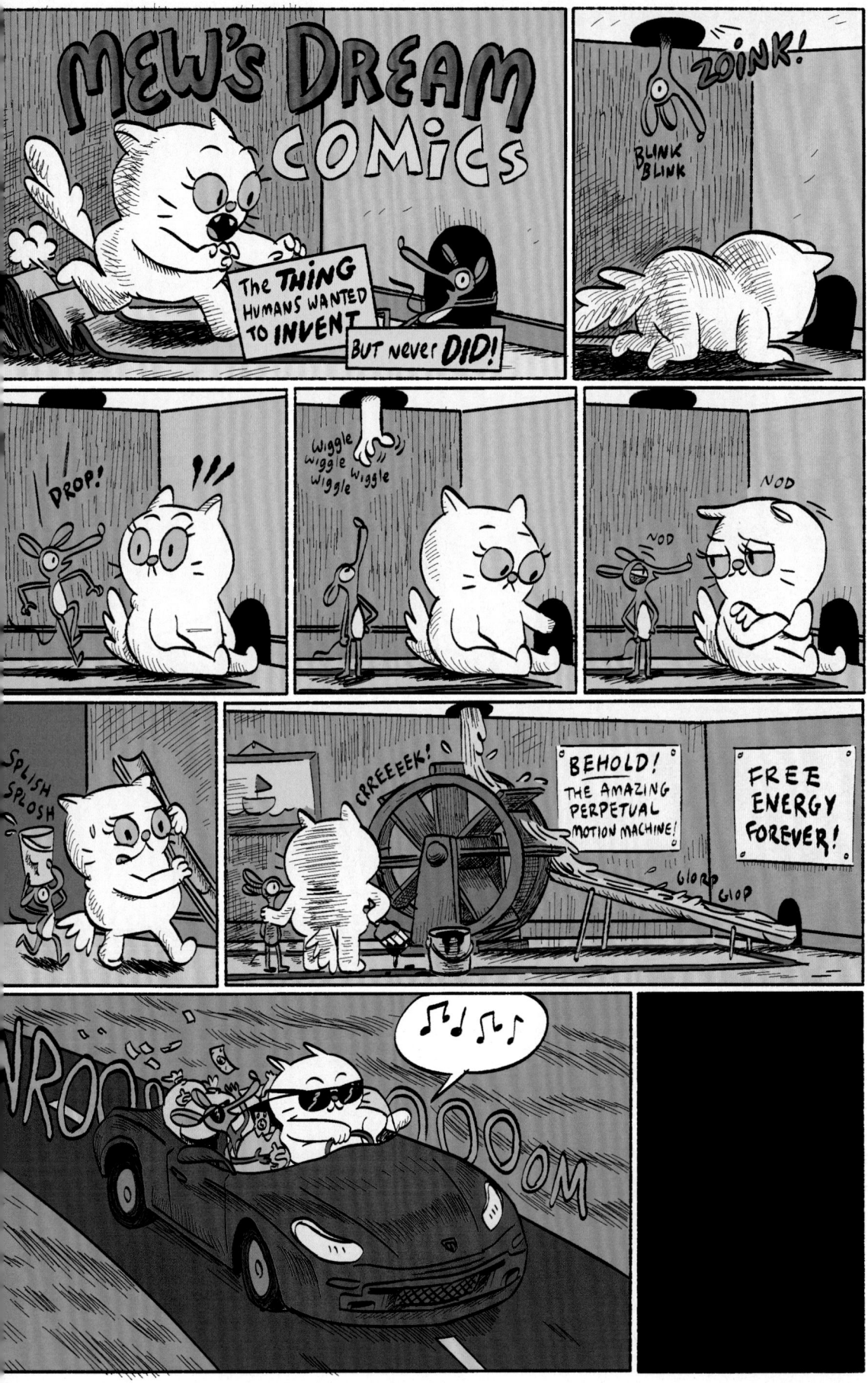
MEW'S DREAM COMICS
The THING HUMANS WANTED TO INVENT
BUT never DID!
ZOINK!
BLINK BLINK
DROP!
Wiggle wiggle wiggle wiggle
NOD
NOD
SPLISH SPLOSH
CREEEEEK!
BEHOLD! THE AMAZING PERPETUAL MOTION MACHINE!
FREE ENERGY FOREVER!
GLORP GLOP
VROOOOOOOOOM

MEW'S DREAM COMICS
TAILS TO ASTONISH!
stuff stuff

SMASH
It's almost charming how you keep trying to fight me, Squirrel Girl, as if I haven't long ago fought someone who can easily defend against squirrels!!
Skreech!!

What the heck, dude?! You smashed right through my wall!!
...Which, uh, which is what I'd say about you smashing into any house and not just this particular one, because I protect this city, and have thus taken a personal stake in all the walls within it??

And go ahead, try to talk me down!
No way, I know your deal! You'll steal my moves and use the same powers against me, talking me into switching sides or something!!
Even with all your powers of squirrel...you're still just a girl. And that means you'll always fail against the Taskmaster.

Hey, here's an idea! Maybe next time don't duplicate the powers of sexist jerks, you might have a better time in the world!

And how to end you once and--
What is the meaning of this?!
Hah! You just stepped in the litter box! Enjoy your foot covered in cat poop, plus the knowledge that karma is real??

This is but a temporary setback! And none can withstand my brutal attacks, least of all you!
DROP
Come on, Tony, we're gonna need wa more help here Answer your friggin text messa

KRASH
SMACK
KRA-KOW
=sigh=

JEAN-PIERRE'S PIZZA
ANCHOVY
SPECIAL!
SMAK
Scree!
hissssss

THANK YOU FOR PURCHASING JEAN-PIERRE'S PIZZA!
Yes, even people without Italian names can still make amazing pizza. Mamma mia! Examine your problematic assumptions while enjoying our delicious slices!!
RRRUMBLE
Taskmaster's taking all we can throw at him, Friday! I'm gonna need stronger armor!
Anyone order a friendly neighborhood wall-crawler?

SMASH
FLING
WHOOSH
KER-
=sigh=
THAK

KRA-KOW

It's child's play to use your momentum *against* you, Hulk, and send you *flying!*
Dodging giant green monsters is among the *simplest* of the many tasks I have mastered!!
RRAAGGH!

KA-SPLASH

SPLOOSH

hisss
SNIKT SNIKT
SNIKT SNIKT

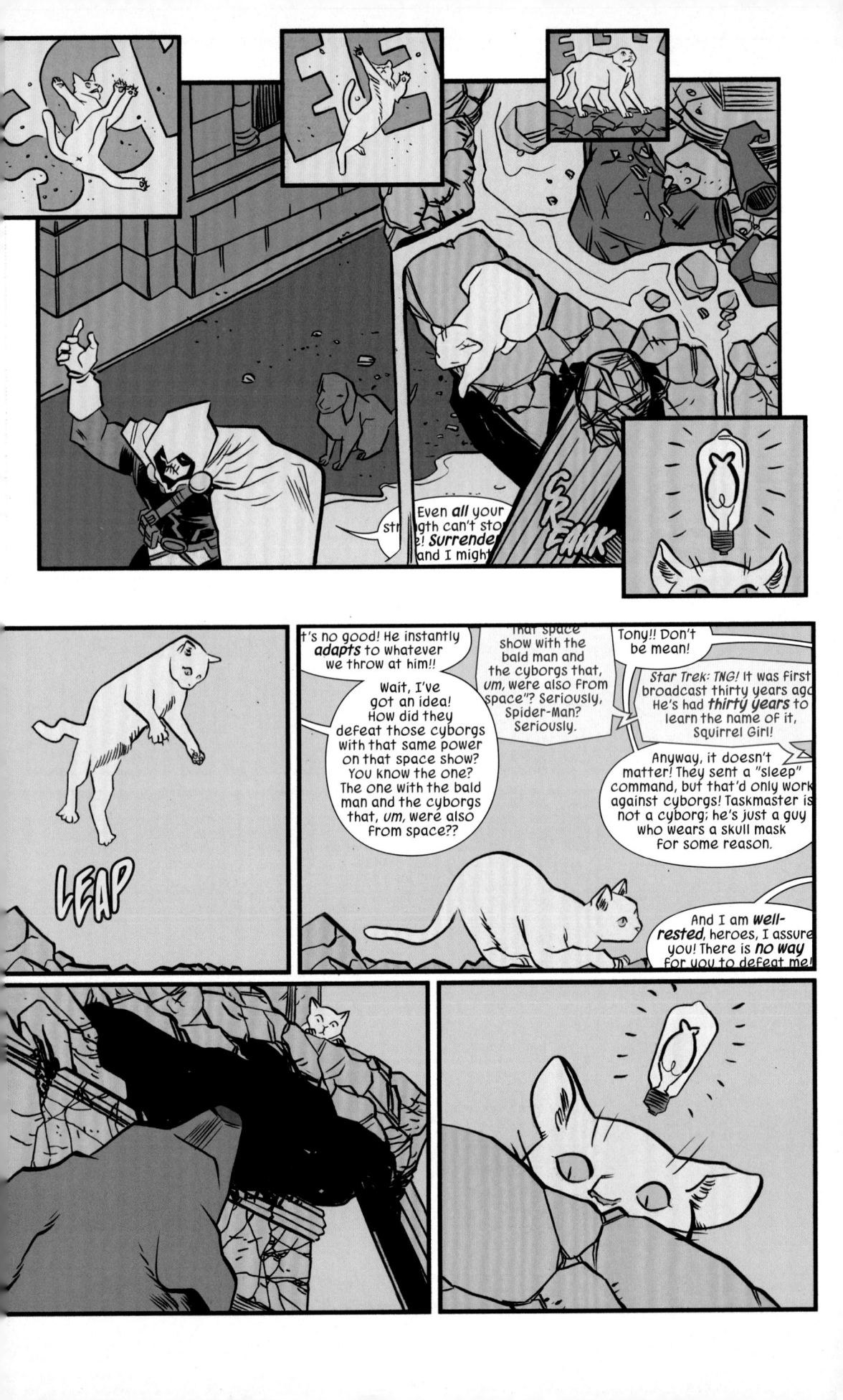
Even all your
gth can't sto
! Surrende
and I might
CRAAK
LEAP
t's no good! He instantly adapts to whatever we throw at him!!
Wait, I've got an idea! How did they defeat those cyborgs with that same power on that space show? You know the one? The one with the bald man and the cyborgs that, um, were also from space??
"That space show with the bald man and the cyborgs that, um, were also from space"? Seriously, Spider-Man? Seriously.
Tony!! Don't be mean!
Star Trek: TNG! It was first broadcast thirty years ago. He's had thirty years to learn the name of it, Squirrel Girl!
Anyway, it doesn't matter! They sent a "sleep" command, but that'd only work against cyborgs! Taskmaster is not a cyborg; he's just a guy who wears a skull mask for some reason.
And I am well-rested, heroes, I assure you! There is no way for you to defeat me!

HOP
HOP
=sigh=
HOP
SLAP

Rarr rarr rarr!
Rarr rarr!
HOP
CRRR
REEEEEEEEEAK
HOP
Rrrrarrr?
Oh, I've learned from the best. Including you, Spider-Man, and how you keep general situational awareness at all times!
POW
THWIP
PLOP
And it will take more than *falling stone* to hit me!
KA-CHUNK

A dog dropping rubble on me?! Another one of your *animal friends,* Squirrel Girl?
UM, JUST BECAUSE I CAN TALK TO SQUIRRELS DOESN'T MEAN I CAN TALK TO ALL ANIMALS!!
NO MATTER HOW MUCH I WISH THAT WERE THE CASE
Rrrwooff!!

Take one step forward, heroes, and I kill the beast.
Everyone, hold up!! He's just an innocent doggo!

gured threatening a *cute animal* would get your attention. You really are *so* predictable.

SMAK

smak
Hey! Knock it off!!

Wretched beast! It'll take more than a tail to stop me, and--
Oh my gosh, OF course. My tail. OF course.
How did I not think OF this sooner?! Thank you, pupper!! You are a good boy!
The one thing you can't duplicate, Taskmaster...
...is my friggin' tail.
Wait!! I--
SMACK
What's that, Taskmaster? Couldn't quite make you out. You were saying something like "Oh, boo hoo! I wish I was born with a tail so I could steal Squirrel Girl's moves and be as awesome as her," right?
I hear it all the time, chump.
purrrr
purrrr
purrrr
purrrr

There you are!!
I've been worried sick, Mew!

an indoor cat. I wonder what she got up to outside?
ust glad she wasn't hurt. That dog was bad enough; imagine if Mew was there?

Hah! Mew versus Taskmaster. He wouldn't stand a chance.
Obviously.
So hey, is my super-powered roommate gonna help me pull together a wall-fixing party or what?

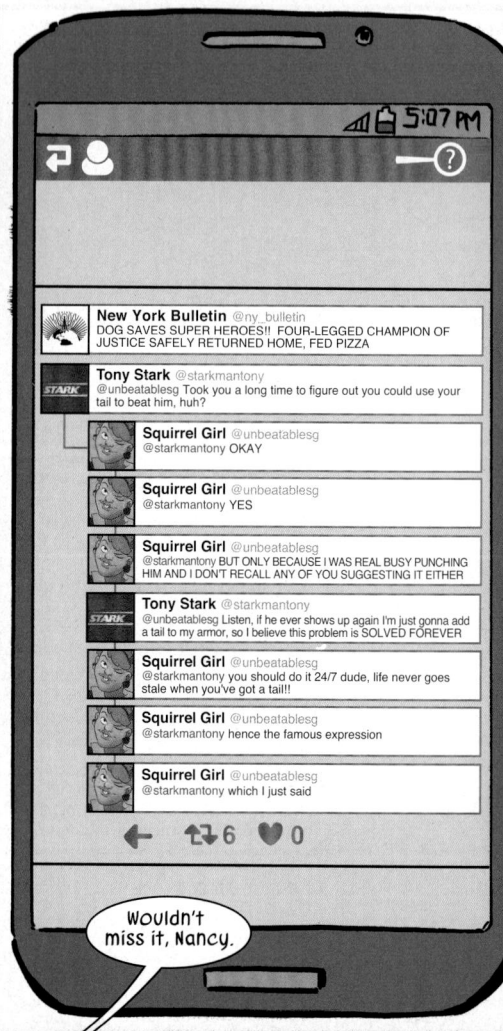
5:07 PM
New York Bulletin @ny_bulletin
DOG SAVES SUPER HEROES!! FOUR-LEGGED CHAMPION OF JUSTICE SAFELY RETURNED HOME, FED PIZZA
Tony Stark @starkmantony
@unbeatablesg Took you a long time to figure out you could use your tail to beat him, huh?
Squirrel Girl @unbeatablesg
@starkmantony OKAY
Squirrel Girl @unbeatablesg
@starkmantony YES
Squirrel Girl @unbeatablesg
@starkmantony BUT ONLY BECAUSE I WAS REAL BUSY PUNCHING HIM AND I DON'T RECALL ANY OF YOU SUGGESTING IT EITHER
Tony Stark @starkmantony
@unbeatablesg Listen, if he ever shows up again I'm just gonna add a tail to my armor, so I believe this problem is SOLVED FOREVER
Squirrel Girl @unbeatablesg
@starkmantony you should do it 24/7 dude, life never goes stale when you've got a tail!!
Squirrel Girl @unbeatablesg
@starkmantony hence the famous expression
Squirrel Girl @unbeatablesg
@starkmantony which I just said
6
0
Wouldn't miss it, Nancy.

purrrr

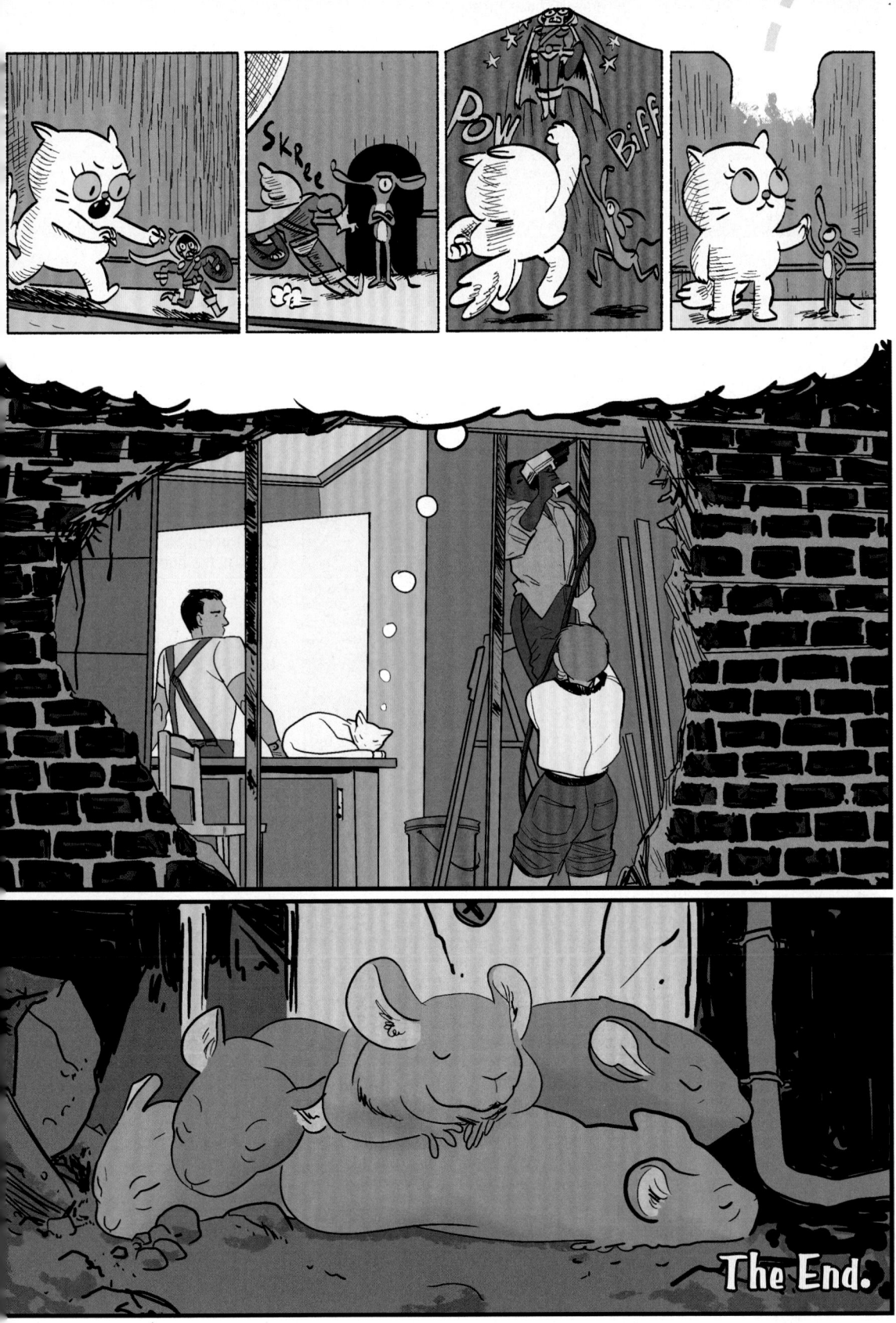
SKREE
POW
BIFF
The End.

Letters From Nuts

Ryan!

Erica!

Send letters to mheroes@marvel.com or 135 W 50th St, 7th Floor, New York, NY 10020 (Please mark "OKAY TO PRINT"

Ryan, Erica and Rico,

Thank you for all of the hard work, talent and dedication you all put into this wonderful, wonderful book each month. It had been nearly fifteen years since I've picked up a print comic every issue without fail, but your book has brought me back into the fold.

After your first issue #1 I made THE UNBEATABLE SQUIRREL GIRL a habit very specifically so that I'd have a box of comics to share with my daughter as soon as she's able to flip through them. I've become assured that I made the right choice for two reasons. First of all, you folks continue to produce an amazing, smart, insightful and funny all-ages comic and you show no signs of slowing down. Second, she's only eighteen months old and is absolutely obsessed with acorns. Every time she goes outside we wind up finding a few acorns around the living room later. Doreen must have some tough-soled shoes, because I swear those acorn caps are worse than Lego bricks to step on.

Nuts to you all,
Daniel and Carolyn Tauber

RYAN: Aw, that's great! I've got a nephew too who just turned three and while he's not quiiiite at the point yet where he's reading comics, I'm really excited for him to start. I am SO READY to be the cool uncle. I've got comics in my house, I've got lots of neat toys and a giant lime green stuffed T-Rex from *Dinosaur Comics* – I AM READY. Perhaps he'll be reading this letter column in a few years and be like, "A time when I was so young that I didn't read comics? IMPOSSIBLE." ALSO: I didn't know stepping on acorn caps was worse than stepping on Lego, but I am happy to take your word for it and would absolutely not like to find out with personal experience.

ERICA: Pro tip: glue down the caps. I learned this from cosplayers and jewelry makers. But yay! I'm glad we could get you back into comics and have provided you with something you can share with your daughter in the future.

Thank you for coming to Lethbridge Word on the Street and the signing at Kapow. My husband and I have been fans of your work for years and are so excited that you are involved in an incredible Marvel comic. I wish we had some better pictures of our Unbeatable Squirrel Boy but he was also very excited.

Miranda
Alberta, Canada

RYAN: Miranda, THIS WAS THE BEST. Your Squirrel Boy was truly unbeatable, and it was hilarious how the second he was dressed up he ran off (because he was shy? Because ADVENTURE BECKONED??). Everyone else: If you've never been to Lethbridge, Alberta, Canada, I recommend it! I went for a walk while I was there and came across HENDERSON LAKE, which I can only assume was named after Erica Henderson, so I instantly felt welcome and at home.

ERICA: That lake thing is probably correct.

Ryan and Erica,

Wow guys, this comic is just swell. Squirrel Girl is truly unbeatable, and Nancy is such a rad character, and Koi Boy and Chipmunk Hunk are undeniably the most perfectly named super heroes ever. And geez, Brain Drain is just trying so hard to be a good super hero and I just...I just want him to be happy. I love you, Brain Drain and I will always be proud of you. No matter what.

Squirrelfully Yours
Elisha Smith
Knoxville, TN

RYAN: Thank you, Elisha! Brain Drain believes in himself and tries his best, and that is all anyone can ask!

ERICA: My only regret is that we didn't get to do more scenes of Brain Drain in his human costume.

Ryan and Erica,

Thank you so much for making me realize how awesome Squirrel Girl is. Your comic makes me crack up every time I read it, especially the "In A Nutshell" segment from Issue 11. It's quite possibly one of the best comics I've read! Squirrel Girl is, thanks to this comic, my favorite Marvel hero. I mean, come on! She's beat up Thanos, Galactus, and even the entire Marvel universe! Anyways, once again, thank you guys!

Ethan

RYAN: Thanks, Ethan! I really enjoy writing the "In A Nutshell" recap pages, and I also like that all the accounts there are real. I would argue it makes total sense that Tony Stark, international CEO and billionaire, would hang out online with Doreen Green. Also if you haven't picked up our THE UNBEATABLE SQUIRREL GIRL BEATS UP THE MARVEL UNIVERSE! original graphic novel (it's an all-new story!), then what are you waiting for? I don't want to spoil anything, but I'll say this: the Marvel Universe does absolutely get beat up.

ERICA: Aw! Thanks! We like her a lot too.

"In this world, even a brain in a jar in a robot body can only do so much." You took the words right out of my mouth. Nicely observed! Brain Drain, Brain Drain, Brain Drain. He's all of it. Were he a man, he'd be my main. He brings the pain! His reign can' e disdained! He brings a presence o this plane that others only feign! If ou mess with him you best be prayin'! eah, like that.

Ryan North and Erica Henderson, you wo are still rocking it like a magikist. Rico Renzi and Travis Lanham and Wil Moss are doing this as well. I'd like to eiterate - this time into lettercol canon that Ryan "Ry No" North should have SG fight a duo composed of the Rhino and a new villaness named the Air-Hen. For no reason I can explain, the latter's given name should be Peppy Bosworth.

Keep it up!
John Velousis

RYAN: John, this Brain Drain heme song is a thing of beauty. And PERSONALLY, I think the Rhino (who s already a Marvel villain, so: CHECK) and the Air-Hen should team up and go on adventures. Erica, do you want to go on an adventure? We are currently n Leeds in the United Kingdom for the Thought Bubble convention, so I guess we're already on one??

ERICA: I love how much people love Brain Drain. It hadn't even been that ong since we introduced him but I was already dying to bring him back. Ryan and I were having breakfast adventures in Leeds. Who can eat the most breakfast?? (Ryan. Ryan can.)

Hello, True Believers,

Thought you might appreciate the Squirrel Girl costume my wife helped create for my 10-year-old daughter Fiona. Happy Halloween!

(And yes, those are totally comics in he background.)

James VanOsdol
Chicago, IL

costume is unbeatable and I certainly hope at Halloween when people opened their doors and saw her they just emptied their entire bowls of candy into her pillowcase. I WILL ACCEPT NOTHING LESS.

ERICA: I hope those bats are year-round décor. Fun times goth house. ANYWAY – Fiona looks great! This makes me happy because I don't think I've seen trick-or-treaters since I left for college. Halloween is not just for rowdy adults, people!

Okay, that's all the room we have this month. DO NOT MISS THE NEXT ISSUE! Why? Because it's a special celebration of the 25th anniversary of Squirrel Girl's first appearance! With a short story by none other than SG's co-creator Will Murray! And you'll maybe (MAYBE!) even learn Squirrel Girl's origin!!!!!!!!!!!!!!!!!!!!!!!!! (And yes, that was twenty-five exclamation points.)

Next Issue:

Attention, Squirrel Scouts! Make sure to check out our production blog, **unbeatablesquirrelgirl.tumblr.com**, where we post behind-the-scenes stuff on how the book gets made, along with all sorts of cool things *you* make: fanart, cosplay, whatever!

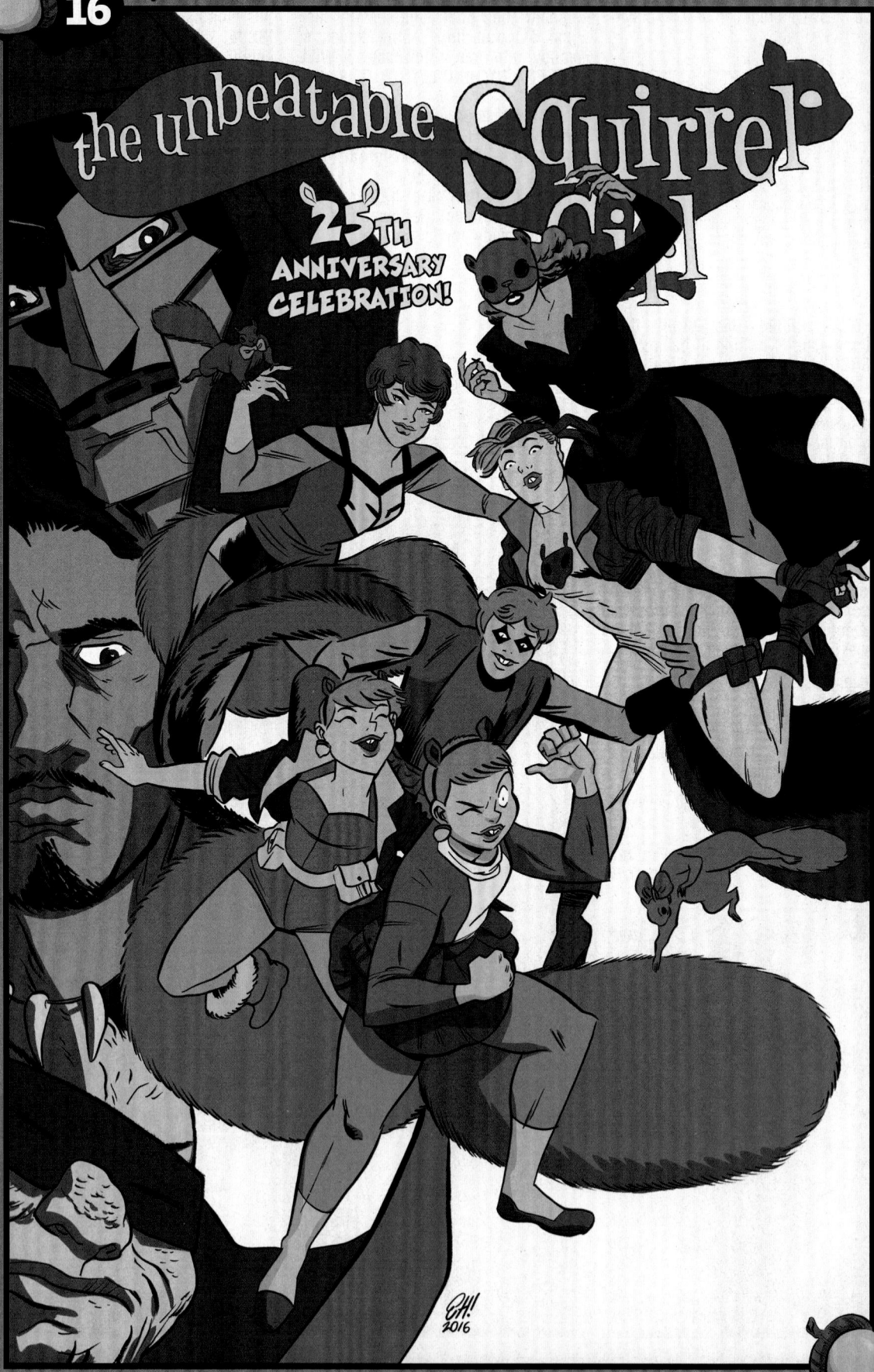
the unbeatable Squirrel Girl
25TH ANNIVERSARY CELEBRATION!
EH! 2016

Doreen Green isn't just a second-year computer science student: she secretly also has all the powers of both squirrel and girl! She uses her amazing abilities to fight crime **and** be as awesome as possible. You know her as...**The Unbeatable Squirrel Girl!** Find out what she's been up to, with...

Squirrel Girl *in a nutshell*

Squirrel Girl @unbeatablesg
IT'S MY BIRTHDAY!! I'M 20 YEARS OLD!! EVERYONE GET REAL EXCITED BECAUSE I WAS BORN...TWENTY YEARS AGO...THIS VERY NIGHT!

Squirrel Girl @unbeatablesg
Fav to wish me happy birthday, RT to wish me an EXTRA happy birthday

Nancy W. @sewwiththeflo
@unbeatablesg Have we worked out the etiquitte of wishing YOURSELF a happy birthday on social media?

Squirrel Girl @unbeatablesg
@sewwiththeflo what if YOU wished me happy birthday, then I could RT that? what if that was a thing we made happen

Nancy W. @sewwiththeflo
Happy birthday to Squirrel Girl, who is both one of my favorite super heroes AND one of my favorite people.

Squirrel Girl @unbeatablesg
@sewwiththeflo aww Nancy!! <3 <3 <3

Tony Stark @starkmantony
@unbeatablesg Are you having a party? Assuming you are having a party, can I come?

Squirrel Girl @unbeatablesg
@starkmantony YES BUT YOU HAVE TO WEAR THE ARMOR

Tony Stark @starkmantony
@unbeatablesg Is this a setup to get me so hepped up on cake that you can convince me to let YOU wear the armor?

Squirrel Girl @unbeatablesg
@starkmantony haha no

Squirrel Girl @unbeatablesg
@starkmantony it's my birthday

Squirrel Girl @unbeatablesg
@starkmantony i'm definitely ending up in that armor tony

Squirrel Girl @unbeatablesg
@starkmantony none can deny me my one true birthday wish

Odinson @num1odinson
@unbeatablesg I pray thee, might Asgardians come to thy party??

Nancy W. @sewwiththeflo
@num1odinson YES BRING LOKI

Odinson @num1odinson
@sewwiththeflo Though I may no longer wield Mjolnir, that does not mean I have been demoted to my brother's secretary service.

Nancy W. @sewwiththeflo
@num1odinson Hmm wow that's a super weird way to spell "yes I will absolutely bring Loki to this party and also Thor, excellent idea Nancy"

Nancy W. @sewwiththeflo
@unbeatablesg I'd be interested in knowing how that little baby born 20 years ago became Squirrel Girl.

Squirrel Girl @unbeatablesg
@sewwiththeflo YES! YES. It is an amazing story.

Nancy W. @sewwiththeflo
@unbeatablesg ...And?

Squirrel Girl @unbeatablesg
@sewwiththeflo And it goes...a little something...A'LIKE THIS.

Nancy W. @sewwiththeflo
@unbeatablesg ...

Nancy W. @sewwiththeflo
@unbeatablesg ...so were you going to post something after that, or

search!

#meetcute
#followtheleaper
#monkeyjoe
#properconcussiontreatment
#fishyhulk
#avengersassemble

MEET CUTE
SINGLES

...she's perfect.
the unbeatable Squirrel Girl

Where are the crossover restaurants that give you both the classy ambiance and the charmingly snooty maitre d', but *also* the crayons and the paper tablecloth you can draw on? "No idea," you whisper, as we both smuggle our crayons and coloring books past the charmingly snooty maitre d'.

THIS JUST IN: Five-year-old Doreen is unbeatably *adorable*, surprising no one.

Geez, it just hit me that the parties we go to as adults *never* have goodie bags that you get to take home at the end!
ADULTS, I HAVE SOME BAD NEWS: somewhere along the line, *we totally lost our way.*

I am happy to report that close reading of Doreen's Thing clock suggests that it's *always* clobbering time. Please, govern yourselves accordingly.

This squirrel learns he can communicate with a new species for the very first time, and the very first message he transmits is "send more peanut butter." This, sadly, once again confirms that it was actually a good idea to not put squirrels in charge of the messages sent into deep space on the *Voyager* spacecraft.

Okay, can we talk about the *Voyager* spacecraft for a second? *Voyager 1* is the farthest object humans have ever sent from Earth, and among the many pictures it's carrying into the universe on a golden record is one of a woman eating an ice cream cone, while a man eats a grilled cheese sandwich, while *another* man pours water into his own mouth. *It's amazing.*

I can't point you to the precise comic where Captain America saves the moon, but I'm certain there is one. And if there isn't, guess what: *I am so ready to write it.*

Hey, what's the new kid drawing?
Haha, who cares?
Shh! Jeremy! This is a quiet drawing period.
And remember! You should draw something that inspires you.
PAINT
That's it for today, everyone! Bring your artwork up to the front, please.
Here you go, Miss Julia!
Uh...

The ~~REALLY~~ COOL
~~GREAT~~
~~UNBELIEVABLE~~
UNBEATABLE
SQUIRREL
GIRL
♫
By DOREEN GREEN

DID YOU KNOW: This part of Doreen's life was written by Will Murray, who wrote her first appearance back in 1992! But then I added these little notes beneath his pages, because we're pals. Yes. I'm almost *certain* we're pals.

Okay, I'm gonna give Doreen a pass here because she's 15, but for *your* information, the best response to a suspected head injury is "call a doctor," not "say 'Maybe it'll wear off' and then get into a FistFight with a super villain." It's not even in the top *ten* best things to do in response to a head injury!

That guy's Emil, and he's an enemy of the Hulk! He's got Hulk's strength and durability, but unlike him, he keeps his smarts while in "Hulk mode" and can *also* breathe underwater. Emil calls himself "The Abomination" instead of "Fishy Hulk" for reasons that I simply do not understand??

IN PARTICULAR, HULK DID NOT BECOME GIANT GREEN RAGE MONSTER SO THAT HE COULD WAIT QUIETLY IN LINE AT THE BANK, AND THAT IS ALL HULK WILL SAY ON THE MATTER!!

This illustrates the Hulk's famous English catchphrase *"Hulk smash,"* which is of course derived from his original famous Latin catchphrase *"veni, vidi, smashi."*

What should we do with this bad-tempered bully?
HULK TEACH HIM LESSON.

Hulk, you can see again! He must've knocked your brain back to normal.
HMPH. HULK'S BRAIN ALWAYS NORMAL!

Hey, there's a big lake north of here. Maybe if you dropped him into it, an ice-cold bath would improve his attitude?

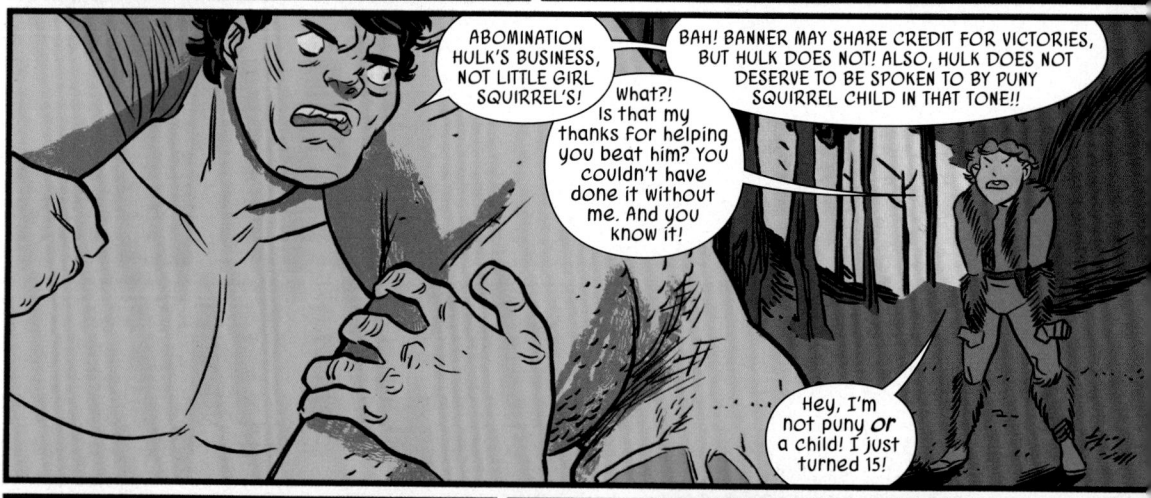
ABOMINATION HULK'S BUSINESS, NOT LITTLE GIRL SQUIRREL'S!
BAH! BANNER MAY SHARE CREDIT FOR VICTORIES, BUT HULK DOES NOT! ALSO, HULK DOES NOT DESERVE TO BE SPOKEN TO BY PUNY SQUIRREL CHILD IN THAT TONE!!
What?! Is that my thanks for helping you beat him? You couldn't have done it without me. And you know it!
Hey, I'm not puny or a child! I just turned 15!

EVERYONE PUNY COMPARED TO HUUUULK!

He's a pretty good jumper, Doreen. Squirrels in his family tree maybe?
You know, I think I'm starting to get the hang of this super hero stuff, Monkey Joe. First I save Iron Man, and now I help the Hulk.
You and what army?

My army!

Dang it I really should've peered through the window before smashing through the wall dang it Red Skull *you know this*

Squirrel Girl did eventually open Loki's present, and once she got rid of the Asgardian Lesser Prank Beast that was making those noises, a lot of the stuff in there was actually really sweet. *The end.*

Letters From Nuts

Ryan!

Erica!

Send letters to mheroes@marvel.com or 135 W 50th St, 7th Floor, New York, NY 10020 (Please mark "OKAY TO PRINT")

Twenty-five years ago this month, MARVEL SUPER-HEROES WINTER SPECIAL #8 hit the stands, with stories starring the X-Men, Drax, Gamora, Namor...and a brand new character named SQUIRREL GIRL!

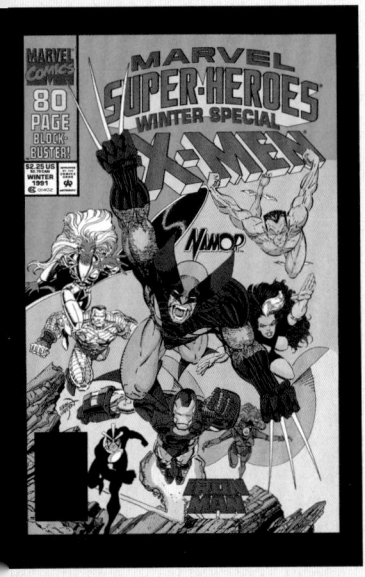

So we're all thrilled and honored to have Doreen's co-creator Will Murray contribute to this anniversary issue by writing that tale of 15-year-old Doreen and the Hulk – such a fun story, right? And we're paying tribute to SG's other co-creator, the legendary Steve Ditko, by running a panel of his art from that original story back on the page where we see Doreen's initial costume design! (So yeah, that wasn't actually Doreen's drawing – she was a talented artist for a 10-year-old, but not THAT talented!)

And TWO years ago this month, THE UNBEATABLE SQUIRREL GIRL #1 (Vol. 1) was released, so we're celebrating that milestone this issue as well! Thanks to all you readers out there for supporting this book like crazy, and for sending us your letters and your photos and your drawings – it's so great knowing these stories are connecting with you! So y'all keep that love coming, and we'll keep telling more Squirrel Girl stories! (And boy are there some exciting ones coming up...!)

Squirrel Girl team,

I couldn't believe it when I read the word "zot" in regards to sending items back in time. I am the only person I know who ever uses that word, despite its incredible usefulness. I'm guessing at least one of you played "Story Machine," that old Texas Instrument writing game with that weird purple hand monster.

Best!
Michele

RYAN: No, I've never played it! But there are few phrases more intriguing than "Texas Instrument writing game with that weird purple hand monster", so COLOR ME INTRIGUED. Since we're (tangentally) talking about calculators, let me say that I do all my calculation on an 37-year-old HP 41-CX, an RPN calculator my dad bought before I was born, and of the type that was used on Space Shuttle missions as a backup way to calculate re-entry if the main computer failed. I mostly use it to add up numbers that are too big for me to do in my head.

ERICA: I've never even owned a fancy calculator, seeing as from sixth grade on I attended arts-focused schools. My frame of reference for "Zot" is the Scott McCloud comic, which is great. There's interdimensional travel there! To a futuristic world! That's LIKE time travel, I guess. Also, according to Google, zot is god in Albanian. We learn something new every day.

Ryan and Erica,

I'd never been into reading comics before my husband put your first issue of SQUIRREL GIRL into my hands. I've been hooked from page one when she starts singing her own theme song to the tune of Spider-Man's theme! (Though, admittedly, I had to look up Spider-Man's theme online so I knew the tune because that's how out of touch I started with comics and super heroes...) Still! SQUIRREL GIRL has made me a comics convert thanks to her commitment to kicking butt but also to solving problems with smarts and friendship. She is basically a huge inspiration to anyone who ever wondered if it was possible to eat nuts AND save the world with some smart observations and a few well-placed butt-kicks!

Your delightful comic inspired my own crafts-building as well, and now I have my very own cobbled-together Squirrel Girl doll crew assembled as well as a crocheted Tippy Toe that I used to make a stop motion of the first scene of issue #v1 that drew me into this fabulous squirrelly world so quickly! I attached a few pictures of the dolls I've made (I even have Nancy in anticipation of future films, wearing a shirt that I hope Mew would approve of!) and here's the link to the short stop motion: https://youtu.be/1otZ-PJcCi8

Many thanks for all you do, can't wait for the next nutty adventure!

April Duclos
Massachusetts

RYAN: April, I love your Tippy AND I LOVE YOUR STOP-MOTION SQUIRREL GIRL RECREATION. My friends and I made stop motion films with action figures when we were in high school, but sadly none of them were a) as good, and b) put on the internet. However I remember one: it starred Spider-Man (um, don't sue me Marvel) and it was about 10 seconds long. Spider-Man said "Time for some heavy reading" and then tried to lift up a newspaper (giant, compared to his action-figure size), and then it collapsed on top of him and he said "Oh no, maybe a little TOO heavy!" I have no regrets.

ERICA: Ryan.

Dear Unbeatable Squirrel Warriors

I just finished 14 and must say, I am impressed with the level of thought that you put into your stories, whether using binary to count on one hand, acting like yelp for Galactus, or physics to defeat Enigmo, Doreen is truly unbeatable. It is great how Doreen and Nancy work so well together!

I have been a longtime fan of SG and am currently working on owning every single one of her appearances, so far I am ten issues away from completion! I am loving every comic you both have put out and know I will continue to enjoy Squirrel Girl's adventures forever!

Ryan, when will we learn more about Nancy? we know so little about her besides she loves Mew, Doreen, knitting, writing Cat-Thor fan fics and maybe has a tattoo?

Erica what has been your favorite panel to draw to date? Is there a character from the Marvel Universe that you would love to draw in a future issue?

P.S. I have enclosed a picture I drew of Doreen and Nancy having a bit of fun!

P.P.S. Just want to finally say that you guys are so lucky working for in my opinion for the best comic company AND the BEST character in the world! keep up the great work Ryan, Erica, Rico, and Travis, I am seriously jealous of all of you!

RYAN: Ah, such a cute drawing!! Besides the fun reveal of FUTURE NANCY in this issue, I also hope we'll be finding out more about Present Nancy soon. Including: NANCY'S MYSTERIOUS SECRETS??

ERICA: Hm. Last issue I got to draw Taskmaster, who I encouraged Ryan to put in a story because he is a skeleton pirate, so THAT was fun. I don't know about favorite panel, but the part that was the most surprisingly fun to draw was the multiple Squirrel Girls vs Doctor Doom fight, which I thought was just going to be terrible because it was like 20 people per panel.

Dear Squirrel Team,

I just read issue #11 (I know, I'm late, it's embarrassing) and, as a Computer Science student, I couldn't resist sending you my opinion in the form of an algorithm.

```
WHILE (reading){
    I_am_mesmerized();
    IF (Doc Ock appears){
        I_dont_realize_its_weird();
    }
}
I_love_it();
I_think_it_is_perfect();
IF (Someone wants to learn about CS){
    I_give_him_or_her_this_issue();
}ELSE{
    I_force_him_or_her_to_read_it();
```

Yours nerdly,
Roni Kaufman

P.S.: I don't know whether I'm the first one to do this. If this not the case, I apologize (another if statement?!).

RYAN: This is great, and I will gladly accept all reader letters in the form of flattering pseudocode from now on!!

ERICA: WHAT IS THIS SORCERY.

Dear Nancy, Doreen, Ryan, and Erica,

I've been a Marvel fan since I was 13 and my daughter Wanda was taught to read with Power Pack comics (POW! BAM! WHAP!). We both absolutely love THE UNBEATABLE SQUIRREL GIRL and giggle maniacally when we read the books again and again. I really like how she solves problems in new and unusual non-violent ways, yet still can appreciate a good butt-kicking occasionally. We enjoyed the Ratatosk storyline so much that we were inspired to do something special this Halloween (see attached pictures). I really hope that Squirrel Girl and Spider-Man can hang out together in the future, and Wanda wants to see more Brain Drain. Thank you so much for all your great work!

Sincerely,
Doug Smith (46) and Wanda Smith (10)

RYAN: Wanda, this part is only fo you, so don't let your dad read this that costume is amazing, there is more Brain Drain in this issue, and we can retcon that to say it was JUST FOR YOU, and thank you so much for being such a great reader! You're the firs Wanda I've ever met AND THEREFORE THE BEST.

Okay Dave, this part of the answer is for you: Doreen and Spider-Mar do (briefly) hang out in the SQUIRREL GIRL BEATS UP THE MARVEL UNIVERSE OGN, and it doesn't work out super well for... well, the Marvel Universe, I guess? But I'd like to see more of that too! She already seems to encounter his villains an awful lot. Also, tell Wanda her costume is awesome!

ERICA: Brain Drain is so much fun to draw. I second this. Also that is an amazing Thor outfit. I'm a proponent of capes as everyday fall wear so the choice of the word "outfit" rather than "costume" was on purpose.

Next: New Costume!

Attention, Squirrel Scouts! Make sure to check out our production blog, **unbeatablesquirrelgirl.tumblr.com**, where we post behind-the-scenes stuff on how the book gets made, along with all sorts of cool things *you* make: fanart, cosplay, whatever!

We don't show the Avengers here because we don't want to *spoil all of Marvel Future continuity,* but let me just say: she's the Unbeatable Squirrel Girl, she runs the gosh-darned *Avengers,* and...Nancy in a building-sized mecha suit.confirmed??

#16 TEASER VARIANT BY **MIKE DEODATO JR.** & **FRANK MARTIN**

#16 STORY THUS FAR VARIANT BY **JOHN ALLISON**

#16 CLASSIC VARIANT BY **JUNE BRIGMAN**, **MARC DEERING** & **JAY DAVID RAMOS**

#16 VARIANT BY **NATASHA ALLEGRI**

#16 DESIGN VARIANT BY **ERICA HENDERSON**